Critical Guides to French Texts

Critical Guides to French Texts

EDITED BY ROGER LITTLE, WOLFGANG VAN EMDEN, DAVID WILLIAMS

VALLÈS

L'Enfant

Pamela M. Moores

Lecturer in Modern Languages
The University of Aston in Birmingham

Grant & Cutler Ltd
1987

Library of Congress Cataloging-in-Publication Data

Moores, Pamela M., 1950-
  Vallès. L'enfant/Pamela M. Moores.

  (Critical guides to French texts: 67)
  Bibliography: p.
  1. Vallès, Jules, 1832-1885. Enfant. I. Title. II. Series.
PQ2458.V7E536 1987 843'.8—dc19 87-23278
ISBN 0-7293-0270-9 (pbk.)

323400

I.S.B.N. 84-599-2172-7

DEPÓSITO LEGAL: V. 2.585 - 1987

Printed in Spain by
Artes Gráficas Soler, S.A., Valencia
for
GRANT & CUTLER LTD
55-57, GREAT MARLBOROUGH STREET, LONDON W1V 2AY
and
27, SOUTH MAIN STREET, WOLFEBORO, NH 03894-2069, USA

Contents

Prefatory Note

All references to *L'Enfant* are based on the Collection Folio edition (Gallimard, 1973), which is currently widely available. It provides an outline of Vallès's life, details of publication of the novel, brief bibliographical advice, and useful notes. Its main asset, however, is Béatrice Didier's preface, which discusses the text in detail in response to the question: '*L'Enfant* de Jules Vallès, roman réaliste ou psycho-drame sado-masochiste?' While some may think the psychoanalytical approach is taken too far, the analysis remains a perceptive and stimulating introduction to the novel.

References to this text will indicate the relevant page number(s) only in brackets, e.g. (p.35). References to other works listed in the Select Bibliography will cite the number of the text in italics, followed by the page number(s), e.g. (*7*, p.48).

1. Introduction

Jules Vallès was born in Le Puy in 1832, son of a teacher Louis Vallez.[1] He was third of seven children born to his mother in a period of nine years, of whom all but he and a younger sister Marie-Louise-Julie died at birth or shortly afterwards. Even the latter suffered from mental illness and died in an asylum at the age of twenty-four. Jules was to be no stranger to suffering from childhood onwards.

In 1840 Monsieur Vallez's promotion took the family from Le Puy to Saint-Etienne, this uprooting exacerbating an already troubled domestic atmosphere. In 1844-45 relations between husband and wife deteriorated, following Monsieur Vallez's adultery with a family friend, and Jules made his first attempts to run away. His father's promotion to a post in Nantes in 1845 provided the opportunity for the family to make a fresh start, but they were homesick for their native province. Nonetheless Jules was performing excellently at school until in 1848 he became involved in political unrest and failed his *baccalauréat*. His father, disturbed by his political activities, and keen for him to excel academically, despatched him to a boarding-school in Paris to repeat the year's study and follow classes at the Lycée Bonaparte in preparation for entry to the prestigious Ecole Normale Supérieure. At the end of the year Jules returned to Nantes unsuccessful, only to compound his father's frustration by failing the *baccalauréat* twice more in 1850. By 1851 tension at home was running high and he was allowed to return to Paris, where he resumed his political activities and failed the *baccalauréat* yet again. In December 1851 he was amongst the Republicans who demonstrated against the 'coup d'Etat'. Monsieur Vallez, in a desperate effort to curb activities which

[1] This was the normal spelling of his father's name. Jules was registered at birth as Vallès Louis-Jules, although his school-records from 1840 to 1845 appear under the name Vallez.

threatened to compromise his career, now asserted his paternal authority. He conspired to obtain a medical certificate declaring his son mentally disturbed, with the result that on 31 December 1851 Jules was interned in the Saint-Jacques asylum in Nantes. Not until the following March, after friends had threatened his father with a public scandal, was he set free.

This is merely a brief sketch of some aspects of Vallès's early years, but to readers of *L'Enfant* it will be sufficient both to suggest parallels between his life and that of Jacques Vingtras and to explain his motivation for exploring in this novel the themes of martyred childhood and abuse of parental authority. *L'Enfant* is the first volume of the Jacques Vingtras trilogy, followed by *Le Bachelier* and *L'Insurgé*. All are based on Vallès's own experience and so knowledge of his life is of particular interest, all the more so as he is remembered not only as a novelist, but equally as a militant journalist and prominent Communard. Students should consult the outline of his career presented in the Folio edition of *L'Enfant*, and if possible the fuller account given by Roger Bellet in the Pléiade edition of his works (*1*).

However, we must be wary of assuming, as critics have often done, that Jacques Vingtras and Jules Vallès are one and the same. Obvious parallels make this tempting, and Vallès does talk of the trilogy as 'mon roman-mémoire' (*4*, p.138), 'mes *Confessions*' (*5*, p.110), and chooses for his hero a name clearly reminiscent of his own, in rhythm, initials and final consonant. Descriptions prefiguring passages of the trilogy occur in the many newspaper articles in which he recalls scenes of his youth and native countryside. Recollections of Vallès's money-box and of New Year's Day in the section 'Souvenirs' of the articles collected under the title *La Rue* in 1866 (*1*, pp.693-700) are both echoed in *L'Enfant*, in the chapters 'L'Argent' (XIII) and 'Les Joies du foyer' (VII) respectively. Also the fact that the dedication of the novel, written in the first person and signed Jules Vallès, leads in to a narrative in the first person by the character Jacques Vingtras further encourages confusion.

However, the very creation of a fictitious character implies that Vallès did not want the trilogy to be regarded as pure autobiography. In *L'Enfant* and *Le Bachelier* he encodes the names of friends and teachers: Monsieur Rodier is renamed Laurier, Lemeignan becomes Legnagna, his friend Charles-Louis Chassin appears as Matoussaint. Also publication in 1884 of *Souvenirs d'un étudiant pauvre* with the pointed sub-title *Mémoires vrais*, treating a period of Vallès's life already evoked in the trilogy, brings into question the veracity of the novels, reinforcing the view that they should not be read as autobiography.

Shyness and discretion are partly responsible, as Vallès reveals in a letter to his friend Hector Malot: 'avertir le public que c'est bien le cœur de M. Vallès qui a été remué par ces misères ou ces amours, cela me répugne et me paraît presque... une trahison' (5, p.60). He also feels some sense of loyalty to the parents he caricatures. When *L'Enfant* was first published under its original title *Jacques Vingtras* (1878), it was signed with the pseudonym La Chaussade and subsequently Jean la Rue. The reasons were not only personal but political. Vallès was in exile in London at the time, and if his works had been presented openly as the memoirs of a Communard, the public indignation which followed their publication would have been very much greater. As it is, no explicit mention of the Commune is made until *L'Insurgé*, first published two years after the amnesty granted to all Communards in 1880. Here significantly the systematic disguise of characters is relaxed, except in the case of Vingtras himself.

Lifelong friends of Vallès, like Arthur Arnould, have maintained that differences between the fiction and reality are only superficial, amounting basically to exaggeration for comic effect. There are, however, significant deviations. Jacques, for example, is an only child. Béatrice Didier suggests that this is a classic example of the insecure child jealously suppressing all rivals in the struggle for his parents' attention (pp.18-19), but this is unlikely since, apart from Julie, Jules's siblings died too young to have posed a serious threat. One suspects that Jules resented his parents' general indifference rather than any affection shown to others. In an early version of *L'Enfant*, in one of his notebooks, he describes the death of Louisou, younger brother of Ernest Pitou (an early incarnation of Jacques Vingtras). Louisou is a sickly child, with a large strawberry mark on his face, and nobody loves him but Ernest. Though the doctor informs his parents that he has not long to live, they obstinately ignore his cries and Ernest's calls for help. The following morning the child is dead and Ernest is overwhelmed with grief and resentment at their harshness. The episode may be based on fact, since Vallès had a younger brother Thomas Jean-Louis, born in 1836, whose death he must have witnessed when he himself was very young. Yet in *L'Enfant* the episode is omitted. The family group is reduced to the basic trio of mother, father and child, to focus on their relationships. When the experience resurfaces, it is in the shape of Louisette's martyrdom (Chapter XIX), thus transferred to another household. Similarly Monsieur Vallez's internment of Jules in an asylum is modified to mere threats of imprisonment (pp.391 and 407), and it is a colleague who treats his son in this manner in *Le Bachelier* (2, p.154). Reality is tempered and manipulated. Vallès spares his parents' reputation, but retains nonetheless episodes which highlight parental abuse. In the notebook Ernest's joyful experiences at Mademoiselle Labre's infants' school are described in detail, but in *L'Enfant* we quickly pass over moments of childhood happiness (pp.47-48) to linger rather on grim college-days (pp.63-69). In reality Monsieur Vallez enjoyed academic success as an *agrégé*, but in *L'Enfant* Monsieur Vingtras is an uninspiring individual, beset by failure. Madame Vallez deserved sympathy, having lost so many children, but in the novel any such extenuating circumstances are suppressed, lest they detract from the portrayal of Jacques's suffering. Chronology is manipulated too.

In short, Jacques Vingtras is not Jules Vallès. *L'Enfant* is a highly selective dramatization of the author's experiences, transposed into fiction in the form of a novel, in order to give universal significance to the central themes. Vingtras is 'un Vallès arrangé pour les besoins de la cause',[2] and a central

[2] See Léon Séché, *Portraits à l'encre: Jules Vallès, sa vie et son œuvre* (Paris, Revue illustrée de Bretagne et d'Anjou, 1886), p.5.

preoccupation of this study must be to elucidate the nature of this cause.

Intentions

In an article entitled 'Les Victimes du livre' in *Le Figaro*, 9 October 1862, Vallès launched an extraordinarily negative attack on literature, condemning the 'Tyrannie comique de l'*Imprimé!*' (*1*, p.230), which he accused of nurturing a debilitating cult of the past, and imprisoning the reader within cultural models which inhibit natural spontaneous behaviour. In these circumstances it may seem surprising that he should have become a novelist at all, and that over a century later students of French literature should study his writing. His very first book *L'Argent* (1857) was in itself a rejection of the literary life, as the full title suggests: *L'Argent par un homme de lettres devenu homme de bourse*. Vallès stressed repeatedly that his aims were social and political not literary. Restricted by the political repression of the Second Empire, he wrote to newspaper editor Albert Rogat in 1867, 'Je fais de la littérature par pis-aller' (*1*, p.921). Nonetheless he enjoyed reading, and the social historians Michelet and Proudhon were formative influences in his life. Significantly the novelists he most admired were great realists such as Balzac and Dickens (*1*, pp.548-59 and *8*, pp.424, 446). In 'Les Victimes du livre' he exaggerates for effect, his real target being misleading romantic literature.[3] This emerges in reviews in *Le Progrès de Lyon*, where he asserts, more positively: 'J'espère faire comprendre jusqu'où, entre des mains heureuses, peut aller l'influence du roman' (*1*, p.325). The writer should confine himself to simple transcription of contemporary life, spurning the imagination and concentrating on his own experiences. Then he may exert a sobering, enlightening influence, confronting the reader with reality rather than offering a form of escapism. This is clearly what Vallès seeks to do in *L'Enfant*. Negative though his view may at first appear, it is motivated by the desire for innovation. To quote Roger Bellet, 'seule une littérature peut

---

[3] Significantly, where Vallès criticizes Balzac, it is for the romantic traits of his writing, for portraying reality 'avec des verres grossissants' (*1*, p.549).

répondre à la littérature; il faut une insurrection de la littérature contre la littérature' (*8*, p.7).

Genesis of 'L'Enfant'

It is in this light that we must consider *L'Enfant*, and the preceding texts 'Lettre de Junius', published in *Le Figaro*, 7 November 1861, and the 'feuilleton' *Le Testament d'un blagueur*, in *La Parodie* in 1869, which are generally acknowledged as constituting important steps in the process of crystallization of the novel. In 'Lettre de Junius' Vallès writes: 'Je vais faire d'une pierre deux coups: vous donner ma biographie et attaquer, par le miroir, une vieille phrase qui court le monde, à savoir: que l'enfance est le plus bel âge de la vie!' (*1*, p.129). The desire to undermine commonplace expectations of an idyllic view of childhood inspires all three texts, but the author's relationship to the child evolves gradually. Writing first under the pseudonym Junius, Vallès further protects his parents by disguising them as aunt and uncle. *Le Testament d'un blagueur* is closer to *L'Enfant* in so far as he now contrives to focus on the basic family trio, yet without exposing his parents, by creating the fictitious Ernest Pitou, and distancing himself from him as the narrator who presents his testament. Also, whereas Junius's letter gives only a brief glimpse of the author's youth, *Le Testament d'un blagueur* is a substantial first draft of *L'Enfant*.

L'Enfant as we know it, however, could not be written before the Paris Commune of 1871 and subsequent exile in England, during which Vallès became more committed to writing a novel than ever before. Journalism, an essentially transient medium, responsive to the contemporary situation, had previously been his first priority. Now editors were suspicious of articles by an ex-Communard. Also the experience of proximity to death in the Commune, coupled with the frustrations of enforced inactivity, made him want to create something more durable, '*écrire* une œuvre, *laisser* quelque chose!' (*5*, p.69). Depressed by England he recalled childhood in France nostalgically, but it was a traumatic personal experience which precipitated his writing of the novel. In 1875 his mistress, a Belgian schoolteacher, gave birth to their child Jeanne-Marie, but when she was only ten months old, Jeanne-Marie died, leaving her father broken-hearted. This kindled Vallès's interest in childhood, and although not published until 1878, the entire novel was written during the year following Jeanne-Marie's death.

Although several passages of *L'Enfant* are taken directly from *Le Testament d'un blagueur*, the two works are different in overall conception. Jacques Vingtras replaces Ernest Pitou and recounts his story directly in the first person. Pitou's experiences drove him to suicide, but this is no longer pertinent, for the prospect of the Commune gives purpose and direction to Jacques's revolt, as Vallès continues his story beyond childhood and on to 1871. The different titles he now considered for the work are revealing. In a letter to Hector Malot on 23 May 1876, he made the following suggestions: '*Enfance d'un fusillé...* ou *d'un réfractaire* ou d'un *révolté*' (*5*, p.101), thus underlining the importance of studying the novel in the light of subsequent developments in the trilogy. The difference between this and previous images of childhood is that rebellion now leads directly on to participation in the Commune (from which Jacques Vingtras emerges unscathed, despite the implications of the first of these tentative titles). Before 1871 Vallès had talked enthusiastically of sketching a vast social and political fresco *L'Histoire de vingt ans (1848-68)*, and after the Commune this project was reformulated as *L'Histoire d'une génération (1848-71)*. However, neither materialized. All Vallès's writing demonstrates that his talent lay in exploiting personal experiences directly, and that objective observation and assessment were not his forte. So it is in the form of the trilogy, an essentially subjective account of events, that his aspirations as a historian and his tendency to self-confession are finally fused.

Outline of the Trilogy

A review of the titles and dedications of each volume of the trilogy enables us to situate *L'Enfant* within the whole. The first volume appeared originally as *Jacques Vingtras* (1878), the second as *Mémoires d'un révolté* (1879), but these titles were modified in 1881 to produce the balanced harmonious sequence *L'Enfant*, *Le Bachelier*, and *L'Insurgé* (first published in 1882). The *raison d'être* of the entire work is revolt against oppression, and the dedication of each volume identifies a particular group of victims. *L'Enfant* is dedicated as follows:

A TOUS CEUX
qui crevèrent d'ennui au collège
ou
qu'on fit pleurer dans la famille,
qui, pendant leur enfance,
furent tyrannisés par leurs maîtres
ou
rossés par leurs parents.

As Vallès informs Malot, 'C'est le procès de la *famille*' (5, p.116). The emphasis is on relationships within the family and on the emotional development of the child abused by his parents. Vallès specifies, 'je m'en tiendrai aux souffrances d'un fils brutalisé par son père et blessé, tout petit, dans le fond de son cœur' (5, p.98). 'Le collège' too is mentioned, for the school is also under attack. In Jacques's family, since his father is a schoolmaster, and his mother too sees herself as an adjunct to the education system, disciplining before loving, the tyranny of parents and of the state educational hierarchy ('l'Université') are closely associated. Monsieur Vingtras lives in fear of the absolute power of his superiors, and reproduces the cycle of intimidation and fear in relationships with his pupils and son. The victim is the child, and his oppressors are readily identified as mother, father and schoolmaster.

Le Bachelier, as the title suggests, pursues the theme of education, but the focus moves outwards from family relationships to the place of the educated young man within society as a whole. The dedication reads:

A CEUX
qui
nourris de grec et latin
sont morts de faim.

The novel is an indictment of a curriculum which concentrates on the classics, neglecting sciences, maths and practical subjects which might provide a better preparation for gainful employment. Vallès's 'bachelier' is the product of a system based on servile indoctrination. Academic success brings him social cachet and high expectations, but in fact he has no alternative but to enter the liberal professions. Elsewhere his education is a hindrance rather than an asset, as it sets him apart from ordinary working people, preventing him from finding work in their midst. In a letter to Malot in May 1879, Vallès summarizes the central thesis of the work as follows: 'C'est farce et sottise, on n'est qu'un blagueur et un fou, d'espérer VIVRE SUR SON EDUCATION' (*5*, p.348). 'L'Université' is accused of dispensing worthless diplomas and creating social misfits. Jacques, as adolescent in Paris, is repeatedly thwarted in his efforts to find a job and make ends meet. Doggedly asserting his individuality despite all, he becomes what Vallès describes as an 'irrégulier', the 'révolté' or 'réfractaire' of the titles proposed above, a victim of injustice and oppression, who resists pressures to conform. Jacques's personal experience of failure and frustration is exacerbated by the repression of the Second Empire, and his revolt assumes clear political dimensions in active opposition to the regime.

L'Insurgé takes up the theme of political revolt and culminates in the exhilarating experience of the Paris Commune. Editing his own newspaper *Le Cri du Peuple* at the height of the Commune, and fighting alongside working-class citizens against the bourgeois traitors of Versailles, Jacques is at last able to express his revolutionary fervour. For the first time in his life he feels a sense of purpose as he joins the Communards in their call for dignity, equality and solidarity. The dedication of *L'Insurgé* reads:

AUX MORTS DE 1871

A TOUS CEUX

qui, victimes de l'injustice sociale,

prirent les armes contre un monde mal fait

et formèrent,

sous le drapeau de la Commune,
la grande fédération des douleurs.

In early childhood Jacques rebels against his parents whom he
identifies as immediately responsible for his suffering, but as he
matures he sees more clearly how they themselves are victims of
the 'monde mal fait' referred to here. In the course of the trilogy
we move from intimate personal rebellion and instinctive suspicion of bourgeois values to wholesale rejection of the socio-
economic and political order. All grievances come together and
are avenged in 'la grande fédération des douleurs'. This
expression appears again in the final chapter of *L'Insurgé* when
Jacques declares:

> Mes rancunes sont mortes — j'ai eu mon jour.
>   Bien d'autres enfants ont été battus comme moi, bien
> d'autres bacheliers ont eu faim, qui sont arrivés au
> cimetière sans avoir leur jeunesse vengée.
>   Toi, tu as rassemblé tes misères et tes peines, et tu as
> amené ton peloton de recrues à cette révolte qui fut la
> grande fédération des douleurs. (*3*, p.333)

These lines demonstrate the progression Vallès seeks to trace in
the trilogy as a whole. In each dedication the extremity of suffering is suggested by the reference to death in the expressions
'crevèrent', 'morts de faim' and 'morts de 1871' respectively.
Yet, as a study of the verbal forms in each case reveals, whereas
the dead of *L'Enfant* and *Le Bachelier* are passive victims,
'qu'on fit pleurer... qui... furent tyrannisés... ou rossés' and
'qui nourris de grec et latin sont morts', the dead of 1871
'prirent les armes et formèrent... la grande fédération', earning
their more glorious fate by positive action.

The emphasis of each volume varies in keeping with Jacques's
changing preoccupations at different stages in his career.
However, as Vallès wrote the trilogy late in life, looking back on
childhood and adolescence with recent experiences of the
Commune in mind, he sought to achieve consistency and con-
tinuity in Jacques's development. His whole intention was to

demonstrate the process of psychological, social and political conditioning which led to participation in the Commune. His thesis was that repression must provoke revolt, and that the Commune was a direct result of oppression in 1848, 1851 and throughout the Second Empire. In portraying Jacques Vingtras he hoped to speak for an entire generation, explaining 'pourquoi il y a eu tant de bohèmes et d'insurgés' (5, p.63), and demonstrating an ineluctable historical process. The mistaken nature of his enterprise is obvious. No general thesis can be demonstrated from one example, and, in any event, Jacques is far from being an average citizen, representative of a generation. Nonetheless Vallès is successful in tracing his personal development through years of frustrated aspirations to glorious self-fulfilment in the revolution, and it is this theme of inevitable progression and fatality that gives the trilogy its unity, direction and poignancy. On these grounds, although this is primarily a study of *L'Enfant*, I shall make brief references to *Le Bachelier* and *L'Insurgé*, where this permits us to see aspects of *L'Enfant* in a new light, situating them in the context of the trilogy as a whole.

This outline of the trilogy has emphasized the theme of revolution, but has not as yet touched upon one essential aspect of its manifestation: Vallès's revolution in style and form. This will be dealt with in the final chapter, where we shall see how the rebellious spirit, evident in content and form alike, shapes an unconventional novel.

2. *Mother and Child*

In view of Vallès's intentions, my study of themes in *L'Enfant* will focus on family relationships as experienced by the child, and other themes will be discussed in this context. Not surprisingly for a lower middle-class family in provincial France of the 1830s and 1840s, it is Jacques's mother who is responsible for his early upbringing, and it is not until he is a young man and the question of his career arises that his father takes much interest in him. Hence I concentrate first on mother and child, and subsequently on father and son. This is further justified by the way in which the novel itself falls into two parts, the turning-point being Chapter XVI. The chapter heading 'Un Drame' suggests the dramatic transformation of family relationships brought about by the discovery of Monsieur Vingtras's adultery with Madame Brignolin. Until then Monsieur Vingtras had spent a lot of time out of the house, but thereafter, whenever he is not at school, he sits at home under his wife's watchful eye. The change radically affects his personality and also confronts him more directly with his son's development. Let us begin, however, at the beginning.

Le fouet

In the first paragraph of the novel Jacques takes us back to infancy and suggests the most obvious form his suffering will take, physical chastisement at the hands of his mother. His dramatic opening question, 'Ai-je été nourri par ma mère?' is prompted by his hesitation as to whether she truly fulfils her maternal role. His answer, 'Je n'en sais rien', defines the stance of childlike ignorance he maintains. However, the evidence speaks for itself. Where others are loved and cherished, Jacques is beaten. A series of caressing diminutives, 'dorloté, tapoté, baisotté', evokes the tenderness of a normal loving relationship between mother and child, but the verb is in the negative — this is not true for Jacques. The onset of a new clause breaks the rhythm as his contrasting experience is introduced. The balanced cadence of three gives way to a stark single verb 'fouetté'. The discordant modification from '-oté' to '-etté' further underlines the contrast. Vallès shows his mastery of language in emphasizing Jacques's deep sense of exclusion, and drawing attention from the outset to the role of 'le fouet', which will dominate relationships between mother and child. It sums up Madame Vingtras's identity as mother: 'Qui remplace une mère? Mon Dieu! une trique remplacerait assez bien la mienne!' (p.146).

Although Jacques exaggerates to intensify the initial shock, there is an obsessional quality about his mother's senseless, routine punishments. They certainly no longer act as a deterrent. Jacques is ready to face the music for a taste of freedom (see pp.41, 75, 255). He appears reconciled to the situation, ironically voicing his mother's lame justification in the repeated phrase 'c'est pour mon bien' (p.47). He recounts how, the more she beats him, the surer he is she is a good mother, engaging in the most tortuous reasoning rather than admit the possibility that she does not love him. Yet the sheer perversity of his logic undermines both his and her credibility. We cannot forget the presence of the word 'mordu' in the opening paragraph, suggesting Jacques's instinctively aggressive retaliation and his spirit of revolt. The opening question itself suggests his alienation and physical estrangement from his mother. But his psychology is complex. He loyally seeks to show respect for her while preserving his self-esteem. His compromise is to go through the motions of defending her, whilst suggesting her faults indirectly. He includes her in his prayers, asking that she continue 'ses bons soins' (p.47), but the ironic ambiguity of this expression is the key to his attitude, for though she clearly does not care for him in the expected fashion, in their relationship beating is a replacement for affection, and is welcomed as a sign of interest and attention. Many passages in the novel illustrate this; disturbed by the menacing conflict which divides his parents on their arrival in Saint-Etienne, Jacques thinks nostalgically of the familiar blows which would at least have cleared the air:

> Je donnerais beaucoup pour recevoir une gifle; ma mère
> est contente quand elle me donne une gifle, — cela
> l'émoustille, c'est le frétillement du hoche-queue, le
> plongeon du canard, — elle s'étire et reconcontre la joue
> de son fils; quelle joie pour une mère de le sentir là à sa
> portée et de se dire: c'est lui, c'est mon enfant, mon fruit,
> cette joue est à moi, — clac! (p.123)

This delightful passage conveys the good humour and vitality
which inspire Jacques's accounts of his mother's treatment. The
psychological reality of their relationship may be disturbing, yet
Madame Vingtras emerges not as a dour symbol of unrelenting
cruelty, but as a dynamic personality who derives active enjoyment, albeit sadistic, from their relationship. Punishing Jacques
provides her with a form of emotional release. Her blows are an
expression of motherly pride, a sign of mutual recognition and
intimacy. When Jacques is mistaken for the kitchen lad at a
children's party, it is only by taking down his trousers and dis-
playing scars from his mother's beating that he convinces her of
his identity (p.78)! Regular beatings constitute normality. When
Madame Vingtras relents, it is during the crisis over her
husband's adultery, described under the ironic subtitle *Chômage*
(p.216). Jacques feels neglected and complains, 'son affection se
détourne. Elle se relâche de sa surveillance'. Later, suffering a
fit of depression, he reflects as to why: 'On ne me bat plus. C'est
peut-être pour ça' (p.269).

One might argue that Jacques is not a victim of suffering since
he actually craves it, inviting punishment in his mother's
interest, 'je sentais bien que cela faisait plaisir à ma mère de me
faire du mal' (p.216). Her sadism gives birth to extraordinary
masochism on his part. When his father's finger is bleeding, he
scratches his hands to share the suffering (p.41). When there is
trouble in his father's classroom, he offers himself as scapegoat
(p.141). His broken arm (p.136) and the broken picture frame
which cuts his feet (p.125) are similarly welcome. He is only too
pleased to suffer if this diminishes and displaces the focus of

family conflict and tension. This point is crucial. Jacques invites physical conflict not through pure masochism, but because he finds physical suffering easier to endure than the emotional distress and psychological pressures which characterize his family life. His suffering is not entirely of his choosing. He simply opts for the lesser of two evils, and it is clear that he longs for a more open and straightforward relationship.

Other mothers

Irony and the principle of opposition established in the opening paragraph allow Jacques to expose his mother's shortcomings indirectly rather than criticizing explicitly. In the course of the novel we encounter a series of happy homes and alternative mother figures whom Jacques contrasts regretfully with his own.

Mademoiselle Balandreau 'bonne vieille fille de cinquante ans' (p.39) is particularly dear, protecting him in early childhood from his mother's punishments. She is even referred to as surrogate mother: 'Ma mère remercie, le soir, sa remplaçante' (p.40), or later, in *Le Bachelier*, as 'la protectrice de ma vie d'enfance' (*2*, p.180). When he returns to Le Puy and is reunited with her, it is like the long-awaited homecoming of a lost son, contrasting markedly with his parents' peremptory farewell and his impatience to leave them (p.170). The comparison is quite explicit: 'La bonne vieille fille m'arrive ébouriffée et émue! et m'embrasse, m'embrasse — comme jamais ne m'a embrassé ma mère' (p.170). It is this absence of warmth for which Jacques's parents, and particularly his mother, are constantly reproached. Also, whereas Madame Vingtras's and Jacques's relationship is exclusively one of domination/subordination, he and Mademoiselle Balandreau do things together, 'ensemble' (p.171), as equals. Even after her death, she remains an ally in Jacques's struggle for freedom, leaving him an inheritance, which is a source of power in conflicts with his parents (*2*, pp.180-81).

In a moment of misery, Jacques expresses the desire to run away and assume a new identity as a negro. His reasons are simple: 'D'abord, les négresses aiment leurs petits. — J'aurais eu une mère aimante' (p.198). To a nineteenth-century French bourgeois reader, this might seem to indicate the extremity of his deprivation, but what attracts him is the prospect of joyful tribal dances and freedom. Vallès highlights the distance between the child's simple emotional demands and his mother's staid bourgeois values. Madame Vingtras and her neighbours look down upon the promiscuous Madame Grélin, but Jacques appreciates her affection and, with the innocence of childhood, knows of no reason to condemn her. On the contrary he states emphatically, 'Je serais bien plus heureux si j'étais le fils à Grélin' (p.46). His own mother has an almost obsessional fear of physical contact, even when beating him: 'elle prit un bâton, un balai, quelque chose qui l'empêchait d'être en contact avec la peau de son enfant, son enfant adoré' (p.132). The belated addition and repetition of 'son enfant adoré', highlighting the contradictory nature of her action, prompts the reader to wonder why she shrinks away. Her love is questioned, though inconclusively. Alternative motives are introduced, tongue-in-cheek, in particular the desire not to bruise her own hand, but one thing remains clear, namely that she is extremely inhibited.

Jacques has no patience with her prudery. If moral respectability is identified with the self-righteous Madame Toullier, he is not attracted: 'Madame Toullier prise, a des poils plein les oreilles, des pieds avec des oignons; elle est plus honnête que madame Grélin. Elle est plus bête et plus laide aussi' (p.47). The unpleasant smells of snuff and 'oignons' (corns *and* onions) contrast with sweet-smelling Madame Grélin. However, it is not physical attraction but kindness and generosity which matter most to Jacques, for we also have the example of the unprepossessing widow, Madame Garnier, with only two teeth, both discoloured. She wins his approval because, 'elle est bonne et tout le monde l'aime' (p.45).

Primness, a sense of propriety and sheer meanness stifle all life and enjoyment in Jacques's home. Repression and inhibition are the enduring leitmotifs. Time spent with the families of Fabre the cobbler and Madame Vincent the grocer provides a moving contrast: 'Je trouve des pères qui pleurent, des mères qui

rient; chez moi, je n'ai jamais vu pleurer, jamais rire ...' (p.130).
When Madame Vingtras is furious because her husband is late to
meet them in Saint-Etienne, her anger is expressed in tight-
lipped stony silence. She stands 'immobile et muette, avec la
rigidité d'une morte, l'insensibilité d'un mannequin et la
solennité d'un revenant' (p.124), this weighty sequence of three
matching nominal phrases underlining the heavily charged
atmosphere of repressed emotion. Madame Vingtras exalts self-
control as a sign of moral distinction, but to Jacques, as the
images 'morte', 'mannequin' and 'revenant' suggest, her self-
discipline is a denial of vital forces, in stark opposition to the
'odeur de joie et de santé' (p.131) in which he revels in the Fabre
and Vincent homes. His parents never allow him to make much
noise (p.46), but here he becomes an enthusiastic member of
'une colonie criarde, joyeuse, insupportable' (p.130). The term
'insupportable' carries little conviction, for our impression of
the Fabre household is one of tolerance and harmony: 'Ils sont
heureux dans cette famille! — c'est cordial, bavard, bon enfant:
tout ça travaille, mais en jacassant; tout ça se dispute, mais en
s'aimant' (p.129). The relaxed, good-humoured familiarity is
evident in the language itself, in the familiar 'ça', the light and
rapid rhythm, the thrust and parry of the parallel clauses quickly
modified. It is a hive of industry, energy and movement, a
stimulating environment which contrasts with the teaching
world. This is a crucial opposition to be examined further in the
next chapter. The difference Jacques perceives is not purely a
function of the personalities of individual parents, but a
question also of professional occupation and social class.

This is borne out on the way to Saint-Etienne. Jacques is
fascinated by a large lady with a plunging neckline who is flirting
merrily with a commercial traveller. 'Comme elle est plus gaie
que ma mère, celle-là!' (p.120) Jacques sighs, and then,
adopting his mother's reasoning, rebukes himself: 'Que viens-je
de dire? ... Ma mère est une sainte femme qui ne rit pas, qui
n'aime pas les fleurs, qui a son rang à garder, — son honneur,
Jacques! Celle-ci est une femme du peuple, une marchande ... Et
tu la compares à ta mère, jeune Vingtras!' (p.120). A blank
space follows. There is no need to elaborate his view of his

mother's smug sense of superiority, implicit in this ludicrous caricature. Here, and in similar passages where Jacques reproachfully distances himself from the first naïve reactions of childhood, he ironically undermines his mother's values which become unconvincing in his mouth. The significant point, however, is the assumption which underpins his mimicry, and on which both parties seem agreed: in her terms, only the common populace stoop to such pleasure; in his, only working-class people show any lust for living.

In a later episode Jacques learns with amazement that Malatesta, the school's leading rebel, dearly loves his mother, despite the fact (or perhaps because!) she is a 'bad mother', who spoils her child, demonstrating her affection with gifts of melons, dates, oranges and secret pocket-money. All is explained when he learns that Malatesta's mother is a pork-butcher: 'Charcutière! Tout s'explique. C'est une femme *du commun*' (p.200). Jacques's mother's peculiar sense of self-esteem prevents her from degrading herself in commercial activity but not, as he bitterly continues, from cowering in fear of the educational hierarchy.

Willpower

Why is it that Madame Vingtras attaches such importance to social rank and prides herself on the distance which Jacques establishes with such regret between herself and other mothers? The explanation lies in her social origins. A simple woman of peasant stock, it is only through marriage to Antoine Vingtras that she has risen to the ranks of the middle-classes, and the lower middle-classes at that. Eager to forget her humble past, she clings obsessionally to her newly acquired status. Her instincts are a product of her peasant birth and education, and as such are to be mistrusted if she is to live up to her new position. On the basis of limited contact with middle-class families, she develops clear preconceptions of the behaviour which befits the family's circumstances. In contrast with simple countryfolk, who learn to respect the force of Nature, she sees herself as becoming part of a more sophisticated civilization and represses first instincts as base and animal. If the families Jacques envies respond to their children's cravings for sweets and toys, it is because they know no better. He feels uneasy at the happiness of the Fabre and Vincent homes (p.132), but his mother's logic ostensibly provides the necessary reassurance. She sees their indulgence as softness and weakness, and proves her own strength of purpose in ruthless enforcement of a stoical code through which she seeks to teach Jacques self-discipline. Hence the importance of 'le fouet' in enforcing her code.

There are numerous references to the notion of rigid rules of conduct. On the unusual occasion when Madame Vingtras hands Jacques a sweet, but promptly destroys his pleasure with her accompanying remark, 'Tiens, mange-la avec du pain', he comments sourly on her ability to encapsulate her lesson in a few words: 'elle sait me rappeler par une fantaisie, un rien, ce qui doit être la loi d'une vie bien conduite et d'un esprit bien réglé' (p.103). When he breaks his arm, and she grudgingly counts the cost of treatment, her concern for economy is attributed to 'les lois d'ordre, qui sont seules le salut des familles, et sans lesquelles on finit par l'hôpital et l'échafaud' (p.137). Jacques may caricature her, mimicking her pious justifications, but there is never any suggestion that she does not genuinely have his interests in mind. She is a conscientious educator, 'toujours sage, donnant la leçon sans pédantisme' (p.160). The expression 'rôle de mère' recurs in Jacques's accounts of her reasoning (pp.160, 276), as do the verbs 'falloir' and 'devoir' repeatedly. Far from neglecting Jacques, she might be accused of excessive zeal in fulfilling her conception of her duty. Jacques remarks wryly, 'Le malheur est qu'elle a une méthode ... comme Descartes ...' (p.152). The disproportion here between the parties compared suggests both her grandiose conception of her role, and the pettiness of her obsession in his view. Yet she is ruthlessly consistent: 'Elle a un système, elle l'applique' (p.203). Jacques cannot but respect this: 'Je suis tombé sur une mère qui a du bon sens, de la méthode' (p.203). The blank space which follows this remark gives us a moment to reflect on the doubtful equation of 'bon sens' and 'méthode' in this instance. Whatever her original motives, the method proves counterproductive when pushed to extremes.

Her aim is to reduce Jacques to meek submission. As she declares in moralizing tones: 'Il ne faut pas que les enfants aient de volonté; ils doivent s'habituer à tout' (p.85). Consequently she systematically frustrates his desires. Jacques loathes onions, so she regularly serves up onion hash. Only when he has learned to stomach the dish, is the routine broken, the purpose achieved (p.154). This is a perverse exercise in power and oppression. However, unwittingly Madame Vingtras seeks to subjugate Jacques's will through a lesson whose very purpose is to demonstrate the importance of willpower and show, 'qu'on vient à bout de tout, que la volonté est la grande maîtresse' (p.154). In the short term she succeeds for he becomes a hardened masochist, spurred on by her single-mindedness and staying-power (p.248). In the long term, however, Madame Vingtras's teaching backfires, for this strength of purpose will also serve him in resisting his parents' will, and temporary repression only intensifies his ultimate revolt.

Another disturbing consequence is that straightforward behaviour becomes impossible. Madame Vingtras, upholder of bourgeois morality, herself presents Jacques with models of deceit, furtively devouring a calf's liver in a hotel kitchen, rather than conceding she is hungry (p.248). Jacques follows her example. He learns to anticipate her perverse reactions and modifies his stated preferences accordingly, yet still she outdoes him. Unpredictably Madame Vingtras decides to indulge Jacques. He says he likes lamb, so he shall eat it. For an entire week she forces a little more of the Sunday joint on him every day in constantly renewed disguise, until in the end he cannot bear it (pp.155-56)!

Subjected to such a constant process of humiliation and deformation, how can Jacques have any confidence in who he is and what he wants? The crisis of identity suggested by the opening question to the novel is scarcely surprising given the disorientating effects of such contradiction and distortion.

Good manners

Other maternal obsessions compound Jacques's confusion, in particular his mother's preoccupation with good manners, which she cultivates as a sign of breeding and social standing. Jacques dutifully enacts a wonderful parody of conventional bourgeois etiquette when he dines at Monsieur Laurier's (pp.219-22). Sitting bolt upright, precariously poised at some distance from his plate, he comes close to falling off his chair several times. (His mother considers such discomfort essential lest he relax!) He is hungry and there is plenty to eat, but he knows he must appear reluctant to accept anything, must wait to be served, must not empty his plate, must not dirty his serviette. Incapacitated by such prohibitions, he is reduced to a farcical clownish figure. Monsieur Laurier despairs, leaves him to his own devices, and Jacques goes home with terrible indigestion and a splitting headache.

His mother's pretensions prepare further scenes of public humiliation. Following private lessons in comportment, the headmaster's party provides the occasion to show off Jacques's newly acquired elegance. After days and nights of feverish rehearsal, under the grand subtitle 'Mon entrée dans le monde' (p.280), he makes his stagelike entry amidst murmurs of amazement, as he glides gracefully across the carpet, ripping it apart with a nail from his shoe! Such scenes take on a nightmarish, almost surreal quality. Jacques is transfixed, performing mechanically, 'un brouillard devant les yeux' (p.282). He carries all his mother's hopes and expectations, and feels utterly inadequate when he crushes them so emphatically.

This scene has its precedents even within the family circle. On his father's birthday Jacques has to perform (pp.104-08). Armed with birthday greetings and a potted geranium, he approaches his father's bed with trepidation. It is almost in slow motion that we live through the crisis, as he loses his balance, his father saves him, and he dangles by the seat of his pants, as soil spills into the bedclothes. Here too we see the debilitating effects of emotional tension. No genuine enjoyment or celebration is possible, and a potentially happy occasion becomes one in a series of humiliating failures.

Dress

The tragi-comedy repeats itself where dress is concerned. A stranger takes Jacques for some form of tourist attraction, and is amazed to find that his clothing conceals a living human being (p.76). Prepared fastidiously by his mother, his clothes owe their eccentricity to her desire for 'un brin d'originalité' (p.358). Her aim is to give him a distinguished appearance: 'Il faut qu'il brille, qu'on le remarque — on est pauvre, mais on a du goût' (p.78). He certainly attracts attention, but her good taste is far from proven by his gaudy costume at school prize-giving (see Chapter V, 'La Toilette'). Clothing becomes a symbol both of Madame Vingtras's preoccupation with appearances and superficial distinction and, simultaneously, Jacques's public humiliation. His mother shows no concern for any sense of personal pride or identity, treating him like a tailor's dummy. Her disregard for his feelings is demonstrated by the discomfort his garments cause, cut from rough irritating cloth, so tight that they restrict his movements (p.77), or so baggy that he is swamped (p.269). They become a material symbol of restriction and exclusion, preventing him from joining in other children's games: 'Et il m'est donné, au sein même de ma ville natale, à douze ans, de connaître, isolé dans ce pantalon, les douleurs sourdes de l'exil' (p.77). One particular suit effects this exile most obviously, for the dye of the material is not fixed, and everyone shies away from him lest he stain their clothing (p.288). Thus clothes themselves become a source of alienation and suffering. Significantly it is Jacques's distinctive hat and overcoat which betray him when he and Madame Devinol are discovered in compromising circumstances (p.330). It is as if external appearances define him, and not his individual personality. This worrying phenomenon is demonstrated when, on his mother's visit to Paris, she can barely accept that he is her son, because he is not wearing the trousers she sent him (pp.356-57). It is not surprising that, as soon as Jacques has the

money to do so, he seeks refuge in anonymity and buys a suit off
the peg (p.394).

Money matters

Thrift is another of Madame Vingtras's foibles, and money
plays an important role in Jacques's family life, as suggested by
the title of Chapter XIII 'L'Argent', placed at the centre of the
novel. It is important to recall that Vallès's first published work
was *L'Argent* (1857), an anonymous study of the Bourse, the
nerve-centre of French capitalism. As a socialist this caused
Vallès embarrassment, and he never openly admitted having
written it. In fact much of the text is technical, and the material
was provided by a specialist, Dervin, but in the preface Vallès
expresses his attitude to money, dismissing idealists who shut
their eyes to material considerations. He had already
experienced sufficient financial hardship by 1857 to recognize
the suffering and bitterness it may cause, whereas money may
free the individual and bring independence. He certainly did not
exalt money as an end in itself, but stressed its importance as a
means of counterbalancing the capitalist threat of exploitation.

In *L'Enfant* Madame Vingtras emerges as a staunch ally of
capitalism, proud to recount her childhood success in commerce
(p.163). Ironically, however, although she prides herself on her
business acumen, the prestige she enjoys on account of her
husband's profession causes her to look down on commercial
activity, and it is only in management of her own household that
she is able to demonstrate her prowess. In Jacques's eyes this
involves rapacious bargaining and public contempt (p.106), and
he is hurt to hear her referred to as the very image of meanness
and obsequiousness: 'cette dame qui marchande toujours ... qui
a son châle collé sur le dos comme une limande' (p.208). Her
concern for profit would be more acceptable to him if associated
with the dignity of earning a livelihood, but she is unperturbed
by such humiliation. She reiterates to Jacques the lesson of
humility to be learned by the poor. He cannot afford to break
his arm (p.136), to complain when he feels ill (p.159), to prefer
particular foods (p.154), but must be grateful for small mercies.
Thus, as a small child, Jacques is encouraged to accept the

situation against which Vallès reacts in *L'Argent*, and which Vingtras goes on to experience at first hand as an impoverished young man in Paris: the power of the rich and the subjection of the poor.

This inequality of rights is mirrored throughout *L'Enfant*. Young Devinol is a rowdy lad, but is not expelled from school because he has rich influential parents (p.317). Jacques, in contrast, has to suffer abject humiliation at Legnagna's boarding school. The deleterious effects of poverty on individual personality are most apparent. Whereas the rich have self-respect, and feel no need to assert themselves, figures like Legnagna, who are humiliated by financial insecurity, seek to humiliate others in turn. Significantly, it is to Monsieur Jaluzot, 'riche de chez lui', that Jacques confesses the heinous crime of copying homework from the classics. Jaluzot scoffs at his scruples, and Jacques observes philosophically, 'on voit bien qu'il a de la fortune' (p.309).

Disputes within the family demonstrate the power money brings. On the journey to Nantes Monsieur Vingtras makes the mistake of entrusting the money to his wife, and is then deprived of refreshment for three days on end, as she exploits her position to degrade him (pp.248-50). When he later discovers her secret savings, he takes his revenge. Now it is her turn to feel impotent and vulnerable, and she soon makes up to him (pp.293-94). On the rare occasions when Madame Vingtras relaxes her control over Jacques, money is the motive, whether she returns to Le Puy to secure an inheritance (p.128), or he is despatched to Chaudeyrolles in the hope of becoming his uncle's heir (p.169).

In relationships between mother and child, money is yet another instrument of tyranny. Madame Vingtras spurs Jacques on with promises of financial reward, but never allows him to take possession of his money. It is piously saved in a money-box to pay for a replacement to spare him from military service — laudable foresight maybe, but scarcely an incentive to a child (pp.159-60). Alerted to her deviousness, Jacques in future secures the promise that he will keep his reward, but still she outdoes him. Keep it he shall, which means he cannot spend it (p.164)!

Possession is what matters to Madame Vingtras. She regards spending money on pleasure as degenerate. The only treat she allows Jacques is midnight mass, because it is free (p.109). When in an unprecedented step she treats Jacques to an evening's entertainment at the Palais-Royal, his pleasure is hollow, when he finds himself obliged to laugh for days afterwards to convince her the money was well spent (p.365). She is so obsessed with thrift and economy, that in her hands money can only be a source of conflict, never an instrument of liberty.

Certainly she does not regard money as a means to impress or command respect. She may well emphasize her sacrifices for Jacques's clothing, but when Monsieur Vingtras unearths her secret cache, she confesses that this is money saved from her clothing allowance (p.293-94). We have seen the painful results for Jacques! For the greater part of the novel he and the reader live under the illusion that the family suffers considerable hardship, but from Legnagna Jacques learns that this is now far from true (p.348). He is indignant to discover he has boarded for a reduced fee, and suffered in consequence, when his parents could have afforded the full cost. His mother is surprised at his disgust. Surely it is better to swallow one's pride and keep the money (p.352). She and her husband maintain the pretence of hardship out of greed, and as an excuse for further humiliating Jacques. Even the money-box turns out to be a hoax. Jacques discovers his mother has broken into it (p.234), but we never learn what becomes of the contents. It was merely an excuse for miserliness. As with the rod, will-power, manners and dress, common sense and good management give way to obsessional constraint and, in this case, sheer niggardliness.

The contrast with the working classes is marked yet again. Whereas the Vingtras are humiliated by apparent poverty, the Fabre and Vincent families are unashamedly poor, with no stigma attached to their condition. Little though they have, they are as uninhibited with money as with their emotions. Jacques is forbidden to give to the poor lest they squander the money. Ernest Vincent is praised for doing so as a sign of generosity (p.132). Towards the end of the novel, when Jacques begins reading revolutionary literature, poverty acquires a new dignity and purpose in his eyes (p.377), but he is already indelibly marked by his mother's obsession. When a collector rewards him with five francs for delivering a kidney-stone, he is overwhelmed. The sense of power and freedom proves too much for him, and initial exhilaration gives way to shame and guilt. A tearful Mademoiselle Balandreau returns the sum, while Jacques suppresses confused feelings of annoyance and revolt (pp.173-74). His thoughts are clearer when his uncle gives him ten francs shortly afterwards. For years he has coveted the privilege of having Moustache polish his shoes, like a young woman yearning for the pleasure of love, yet reluctantly forgoing it (pp.86-87). The comparison is Jacques's. It suggests the notion of sinful indulgence he associates with spending money on a luxury — a legacy of his mother's puritanical rigour. Away from her watchful eye, he now calls upon Moustache's services every morning (p.183). It is not that he seeks to dominate, but he craves the right to assert his independence and command respect. Money may bring this sense of dignity, as Jacques realizes increasingly in the latter part of the novel. His father, resenting his educational failures, begrudges the cost of keeping and educating him. He is made to feel painfully indebted to his parents (p.391), and this is yet another contributory factor to his overwhelming sense of inadequacy.

Emasculation

We have seen Jacques deprived, repressed, denatured, dressed ridiculously, behaving foolishly. Béatrice Didier (p.21) suggests that Madame Vingtras's process of humiliation is sexual in nature: a form of castration, illustrated poignantly in Chapter XII, when we see Jacques in his apron, washing dishes and doing housework. His passion for polishing is described as 'monomanie frottante' (p.153). Imprisoned like a housemaid, frustrated in his aspirations, this is his only way to express his virility. Later in the chapter we see him a victim of his mother's puritanical obsession with cleanliness. Presented in association with episodes focusing on Jacques's physical appetites (alimentary and sexual), the bath scene too assumes sexual overtones which are confirmed by the almost hallucinatory quality of Jacques's highly metaphorical description. Béatrice Didier (pp.23-24) comments in some detail on this passage, in which Madame Vingtras, bucket in hand, pursues Jacques, who takes on the role of the goddess Galatea (p.157). His emasculation is reiterated by his reflection in the mirror 'pudique dans mon impudeur ... nu comme un amour, cul-de-lampe léger, ange du décrotté', each qualification exposing him as an innocuous asexual figure. The following paragraph reinforces this impression, though in a different vein, as Jacques compares himself to the bloodless flesh of veal on the butcher's slab. Whereas the Fabre and Vincent children enjoy the freedom to assert themselves, to mess about and get dirty (pp.128-31), he is denuded, reduced to a pale effeminate figure, a plaything in his mother's hands. It is she who violates him: 'Et les oreilles! ah! les oreilles! On tortillait un bout de serviette et l'on y entrait jusqu'au fond, comme on enfonce un foret, comme on plante un tire-bouchon ...' (p.157). The line trails away, leaving us to pursue the notion of sexual penetration and the reversal of sexual roles, as mother dominates child. It is because Madame Vingtras feels so unequal to her social role that she is so assertive, that she indulges in eccentric exhibitionism, clumsy dancing displays, and proud parading of her thick Auvergne accent (pp.286-91). Masochist that he is, Jacques may be reconciled to personal embarrassment, but his mother's eccentricities distress him. Although she prides herself on unrelenting observation of her principles, she can be pitifully inconsistent. As they dine in Tours, she gives Jacques a lesson on manners while stuffing leftovers into her bag, and then rebukes him for blushing (p.258)! His self-respect is already at a low ebb. We have seen him describe himself as a dwarf (p.77), an infirmity (p.81), as ugly and slovenly (p.104). To be dominated by such a figure of mockery only reinforces this sense of inadequacy.

Nonetheless, judging by the interest young ladies take in Jacques, he develops into a handsome young man, whose company flatters Madame Devinol. His mother is suprised. She still regards him as a child, and when prompted to reflect on his appearance, thinks of his fat tummy (pp.317-18). It is not until he has enjoyed some independence in Paris, that she becomes conscious of his strength, the newly grown moustache — the signs of manhood. 'C'est que tu es beau garçon, sais-tu!' she exclaims (p.351). Previously it has always been his shortcomings she has noted, but now she is proud and, revealingly, remarks on their physical resemblance, whereas so often in the past she has virtually disowned him. Although she thus recognizes him as her child, she acknowledges his manhood. From this point onwards their relationship will evolve on an entirely different basis. His days of subordination to her whims are over.

Until this point, however, repression dominates. In every aspect of Jacques's life, his mother denies him the freedom to act naturally, express his feelings and discover his own identity. Her domination is total, and his rights are entirely ignored. The source of all Jacques's suffering, whether physical or psychological, is attributed to this fundamental lack of liberty. Vallès's suspicion of literature was voiced as fear of a source of tyranny. His response is to reiterate incessantly in his writing the values of freedom, naturalness and spontaneity. Jacques's reaction is anticipated in the call repeated so often in Vallès's journalism, to be defiant and assert one's individuality despite all: 'Il faut à tout prix réagir et exalter la personnalité en haine de l'enrégimentation' (*8*, p.284). Undeniably Jacques develops a highly distinctive rebellious personality as a result.

3. Like Father Like Son?

Antoine Vingtras's relatives are simple peasants and craftsmen except his uncle, local priest of Chaudeyrolles, but even he lives on the land and remains part of the rural community and a long-established patriarchal order. In contrast Antoine demonstrates ambition and perseverance, embarking on a teaching career, and distancing himself from his roots both socially and geographically. Ironically his sacrifices are more obvious than his rewards. As 'pion' in Le Puy, he is on the bottom rung of the ladder, as the family are repeatedly reminded. Jacques looks on helplessly as older pupils make fun of his father (pp.64-65). When he himself dares to retaliate against the attacks of a teacher's son, the mother is outraged: 'Si maintenant les fils de pion assassinent les fils de professeur!' (p.97). Jacques is the one to be punished by the headmaster, whose main concern is to preserve the tyrannical hierarchy to which teacher and pupil alike are subjected.

Vallès is clearly inspired by the treatment his own family received at the hands of the University. In 1833 his father was dismissed from a state school in Le Puy, because the Principal was dissatisfied with his work. He spent the following years working in a private school and reapplying in vain for reinstatement. When he was eventually readmitted into the state system in the late thirties, it was in a temporary capacity, and not until the move to Saint-Etienne in 1840 did he gain a permanent post. In 1845, although he did well in the written part of the agrégation, his oral let him down. Not until the summer of 1846 was he finally successful. However, even academic qualifications did not bring security. The French schoolmaster during this period was in a precarious position. Between 1849 and 1853 when Louis Vallez was teaching in Nantes, inspectors submitted unfavourable reports on his work. He had to tread carefully.

This is the situation reflected in the novel, as husband and wife demean themselves to please. If Monsieur Vingtras strays from the straight and narrow, he is promptly admonished by the headmaster. The lesson of self-effacement and subservience is one the whole family has to learn.

Monsieur Vingtras's domestic situation reinforces his subordination. His wife shows respect for his rank and position, but not his person. She even dictates relationships between father and son, as we see on Antoine's birthday (pp.104-08). Henpecked at home, humiliated at school, Monsieur Vingtras is brought closer to his son by their common suffering. When they look to one another as friend and ally, these are moments Jacques cherishes dearly. After a difficult night in Orléans, they celebrate with a colleague, Chanlaire, while Madame Vingtras sleeps, incapacitated with indigestion and migraine. Jacques, flattered at being regarded as an equal, remarks, 'C'est la première fois que je suis camarade avec mon père, et que nous trinquons comme deux amis' (p.253). Until now, only Mademoiselle Balandreau, uncles and cousins have shown him such respect. Chanlaire's presence gives Monsieur Vingtras courage, but Madame Vingtras's absence is the determining factor. As soon as she wakes up, the normal hierarchy is restored.

Béatrice Didier describes the novel as 'ce roman de l'enfermement' (p.10). Both Jacques and his father are stifled and imprisoned at home and school. The image of the prison appears in the very first chapter of the novel. The local gaoler takes Jacques out sometimes to cheer him up. They go to the prison 'parce que c'est plus gai' (p.42)! The parallel is also established between prison and school (p.63). Similarities between the educational process and the penal system are repeatedly confirmed. Jacques is locked up for hours on end (pp.144-45). His life becomes an interminable series of punishments: 'Je ne suis plus qu'une bête à pensums! Des lignes, des lignes! — des arrêts et des retenues, du cachot!' (p.193). Staff and pupils alike are depicted as prisoners (pp.65-66), and when Jacques talks of running away from Legnagna's, it is as 'un évadé du bagne' (p.343).

Father and son are crippled emotionally by constant

repression. Whenever they reach out for reassurance, or even a simple greeting, the result is awkward encounters verging on the farcical, as when Monsieur Vingtras greets his wife and child in Saint-Etienne: '(Il tend les bras vers ma mère et la manque) ... Il va pour m'embrasser à mon tour, il me rate; comme il a raté ma mère. Pas de chance pour les embrassades, pas de veine pour les baisers' (p.121). Later in the cab, when Jacques bends forward, his head collides with his father's: '*pan*! — Nous nous cognons — nous nous relevons comme deux Guignols! — Encore un faux mouvement — *pan, pan*! — c'est en mesure' (p.122). These are the pathetic, clumsy movements of poorly operated puppets.

Self-assertion outside the home

In order to satisfy their emotional needs, Jacques and his father look outside the home — a condemnation of the family, which both see only as a source of oppression from which they long to escape.

For Jacques, self-assertion takes a variety of forms. He is fascinated by the adventures of Robinson Crusoe and dreams of emulating him (Chapter XV, 'Projets d'évasion'). Fights with other boys provide another emotional outlet. His thirst for physical conflict can be traced throughout the trilogy, from Uncle Joseph's lessons on combat (p.55) and childhood scuffles (p.97) onwards. When a pub brawl erupts between local villagers and outsiders, Jacques longs to join the fray (p.100). At school he eagerly defends a reputation for strength and courage (p.142). He likes to be the leader of the gang (p.184). This longing to assert himself physically culminates in the duel of the final chapter, the first in a series of duels, which are presented as cathartic liberating experiences, steps on the path to the ultimate combat of the Commune.

At the opposite extreme Jacques savours moments of silence and tranquillity, when he is master of his own emotions, lost in thought in the peace of the countryside with La Polonie (p.62) or his cousins (p.188). He even welcomes detentions (p.193), or returns early to the dormitory at Legnagna's (p.339), in order to enjoy precious moments of uninterrupted privacy. Solitude is bliss, because he can simply be himself.

It is love, however, which he and his father crave above all. Mademoiselle Balandreau may satisfy Jacques's needs as a child, but increasingly, as he grows up, he follows his father's lead in pursuing romantic adventures. In Saint-Etienne the telltale orange-peel and a conspiratorial conversation with a colleague suggest how Monsieur Vingtras has enjoyed his wife's absence (pp.125-27). His subsequent adultery with Madame Brignolin confirms his betrayal (Chapter XVI). Significantly, in the Brignolin, Grélin and Vincent homes, the breakdown in conjugal relationships appears to foster rather than inhibit spontaneous affection and enjoyment. Madame Brignolin is the very antithesis of Madame Vingtras: seductive, sensual, feminine. She dotes on her children, and her philosophy is compelling: 'Il faut que tout le monde s'amuse!' (p.214). Even Madame Vingtras complies (until she discovers her husband's adultery!) while both Monsieur Grélin and Monsieur Brignolin, pathetic figures preoccupied with their professions, seem unperturbed by their wives' independence. Love is depicted as an instinctive emotion to be found outside institutionalised relationships, untrammelled by bourgeois morality.

Jacques experiences an exhilarating form of liberation in sensual indulgence, and the novel traces a number of encounters with members of the opposite sex who arouse his desire. When Uncle Joseph marries Célina Garnier, Jacques is passionately jealous. Even though at this age he apparently still thought babies were born under cabbages, he trembles at her touch (pp.56-57). His recollections of Apollonie during the same period focus on sensual impressions evoking physical desire (pp.58-62). Riding on horseback behind her fills him with self-respect, which he longs to experience again when he becomes infatuated with the circus performer Paola, whose eyes meet his as he attempts to pick up her whip (p.115). Not surprisingly, given its role in his relationship with his mother, the whip exerts a special fascination, but Jacques's reactions are recounted in apparent innocence, as are his naïve remarks about the mystery of human procreation (pp.57, 133-34, 182). Nonetheless there is the suggestion that repression merely exacerbates curiosity, and, in the case of the whip, may pervert.

Adolescent diffidence follows, as demonstrated by Jacques's embarrassment on meeting a childhood friend Mademoiselle Perrinet (p.172), or his two cousins (p.185). His behaviour ranges from bold exhibitionism to bashful blushes, but he is blissfully happy with his cousins: 'Nous sommes heureux, heureux comme je ne l'ai jamais été, comme je ne le serai jamais' (p.186). He and Marguerite fall in love, and he keeps her bouquet in memory of an interval of happiness beyond his parents' control (p.191). His mother recognizes the threat it poses, and destroys it savagely while her husband looks on (pp.303-04). Jacques sympathizes with his father and never condemns his infidelity, but this support is not reciprocated. After the Brignolin affair Monsieur Vingtras is so embittered that he begrudges Jacques the slightest happiness.

Jacques's seduction by Madame Devinol marks his coming of age sexually (p.329). Their relationship introduces him to the enchanting world of the theatre, in a whirlwind of emotional and sensual experience (p.321). He enjoys their intimacy and confides in Madame Devinol the misfortunes of his troubled childhood. She becomes a secret ally, a substitute mother and lover simultaneously. Yet his parents do not enquire too far, flattered by his association with a wealthy middle-class mother. Even when the relationship is exposed, there is no family scene, and Jacques is packed off to Paris without any fuss (p.330). Comparisons with his father's love affair are inevitable. Both men cherish rare moments of pleasure in a relationship from which Madame Vingtras is excluded. Yet the comparison also attracts attention to their different positions. Whereas for Jacques the ensuing scandal opens the gateway to freedom, for his father the prison walls close in on him after his confrontation with his wife.

The conflict prevents any further friendship between father and son, and entirely alters relationships within the family, as Jacques explains: 'Mon père, depuis ce jour-là (est-ce la fièvre ou le remords, la honte ou le regret?), mon père a changé pour moi ... Mon père a besoin de rejeter sur quelqu'un sa peine et il fait passer sur moi son chagrin, sa colère. Ma mère m'a lâché, mon père m'empoigne' (pp.227-28). Whereas Madame Vingtras had been an entertaining taskmaster, her husband's sadism is mournful and unrelenting. The parental roles are reversed, and what would previously have seemed impossible occurs: Madame Vingtras becomes Jacques's ally, intervening to stop her husband's barbaric beating (p.230).

Rejection of his father's path

Jacques is now alienated from his father, yet feels partly responsible for his misery. The headmaster has warned Monsieur Vingtras not to continue seeing Madame Brignolin and suggested he devote his energy to improving his son's academic performance. Jacques is led to believe he has failed his father, and tackles his studies with zeal in an effort to compensate. In fact he is merely a scapegoat, as on previous occasions (e.g. pp.40-41). Nonetheless there are fundamental reasons for his recurring sense of guilt. It may be his mother who exerts the formative influence at home, but it is his father who provides the model he is pressured to emulate and which he rejects so wholeheartedly.

From the beginning of the novel an opposition is established between the simple contentment of peasants and workers, and the dull, petty preoccupations of schoolmasters. The contrast is present in our first introduction to the family in Chapter II, when Uncle Joseph asks his nephew if he is happy in the company of his father's friends and Jacques responds emphatically, 'Oh! mais non!', as he recalls boring meals in their company (p.55). This contrasts with the admiration which permeates his description of Uncle Joseph, a carpenter, and a large handsome man (p.54). Jacques is very conscious of his physical presence, warmth and vitality, as he throws him playfully into the air, or reads him stories in bed. He takes him everywhere and Jacques crawls from lap to lap in the craftsmen's club, while they drink merrily, or watches Joseph working and singing late into the night. Never do we see such intimacy between father and son. The only comparable relationship is with Jacques's great uncle of whom he reflects wistfully, 'Oh! s'il eût été mon père, cet oncle au bon cœur!' (p.182).

The contrast re-emerges when Jacques is with the cobbler's family in Saint-Etienne. He himself draws attention to the parallel between the children's big brother and Uncle Joseph (p.128). Both men are skilled craftsmen and members of their guild. Jacques shares their pride in their work. Their ribbons of honour and 'chefs-d'œuvre' are visible signs of their achievement. Yet they are also relaxed and unpretentious in a healthy and stable environment. The individual's occupation appears to determine his whole lifestyle and personality. The farmworkers and their families too (Chapter VI 'Vacances' and Chapter XIV 'Voyage au pays') lead an idyllic life in harmony with Nature. There is never any mention of hostile elements or damaged crops, but an atmosphere of plenty and carefree enjoyment. This contrasts with the dark damp school buildings and the hostile atmosphere which pervades even the teacher's home. Here we find only stinginess and tension. The underlying suggestion is that manual work satisfies physical needs and the craftsmen's skill enhances self-respect, whereas the rigid mental discipline of the nineteenth-century French curriculum is merely inhibiting. Success is not lightly acknowledged and, as we have seen, Monsieur Vingtras confronts repeated frustration and degradation. Nor is he presented as an exception. His colleague Monsieur Bergougnard, 'homme osseux, blême, toujours vêtu sévèrement' (p.295), epitomizes the ruthless severity and sickly restriction inbred by the profession. He ties himself in such knots with his arguments that he is thoroughly constipated both mentally and physically (p.296). As is the case first for Madame Vingtras, and subsequently her husband, Bergougnard's physical activity is confined to abusing his children. It is his daughter Louisette who becomes the tragic symbol of child martyrdom in the novel, whilst the homes of artisans and peasants provide contrasting images of freedom and happiness.

Jacques's parents want him to follow in his father's footsteps: 'ma mère me fait donner de l'éducation, elle ne veut pas que je sois un campagnard comme elle! Ma mère veut que son Jacques soit un *Monsieur*' (p.94). In Jacques's eyes the alternatives are clearly defined, as is his instinctive preference: '... je préférerais

des sabots! j'aime encore mieux l'odeur de Florimond le
laboureur que celle de Monsieur Sother, le professeur de
huitième: j'aime mieux faire des paquets de foin que lire ma
grammaire, et rôder dans l'étable que traîner dans l'étude'
(p.95). Inevitably, as a child, he is attracted by open enjoyment
and practical activity, rather than vague notions of social
prestige and academic distinction. Yet, because his parents
invest such emotional energy in their ambitions, he suppresses
his feelings guiltily (p.95). Time and time again we see him
mentally comparing the two worlds, the loose, comfortable
garments of the peasants, openly stained and discoloured, as
opposed to his father's tight trousers, meticulously mended, yet
threadbare and fragile (pp.95-96). The peasants' confidence
contrasts with his shame and fear, their merriment with his
misery. Yet it is not until his mother's trip to Paris, after his
disastrous year at Legnagna's, that Jacques dares to blurt out
the truth — his desire to learn a trade, and become a worker:
'Oui, je veux entrer dans une usine, je veux être d'un atelier, je
porterai les caisses, je mettrai les volets, je balaierai la place,
mais j'apprendrai un métier' (p.367). Despite his mother's
attempts to play on his sense of duty, he remains defiant: 'Ce
que je veux, c'est ne pas prendre sa profession, un métier de
chien savant!... J'aime mieux une veste comme mon oncle
Joseph, ma paye le samedi, et le droit d'aller où je veux le
dimanche' (p.367). The blank space and line of dots which
follow this passage underline its importance. In *Le Bachelier*
similarly we see Jacques constantly torn between his desire to
find a job amongst ordinary workers and the openings readily
available to him in the teaching profession.

Monsieur Vingtras evidently finds it difficult to come to terms
with his own situation; hence his cruelty and bitterness. As a
result the one thing that Jacques knows is that he will not follow
the same path. The confrontation emerges at this point not
simply because of his failure in competitive examinations, for
events leading up to the *Concours Général* remove any
motivation to excel. Jacques has nothing but contempt for
Legnagna's cramming institution. The only point in his winning
a prize would be to pay off his debt to the school (p.344).

However, any such desire is overridden by the momentous impact of a pathetic routine he witnesses on the way to the Sorbonne as a former teaching assistant painstakingly launders his handkerchief on the banks of the Seine (p.345). This scene of degradation haunts Jacques all day, preventing him from concentrating on the examination, and bringing matters to a head. There is no point in performing well if it is simply to condemn himself to such a life of misery like his father, no point either in prolonging the charade.

Critique of the education system

Reactions to the education system are thus central to the rift between father and son. The dedication of the novel specifically mentions boredom 'au collège' and the tyranny of 'maîtres'. In autobiographical writing and journalism alike, education was always an important theme for Vallès. In March 1871, when elected to the Commune, he became a member of the Commission for Education. He passionately believed that the philosophy underlying formal education required thorough re-examination. Jacques reflects his views, instinctively questioning the rigid hierarchy, the teaching and curriculum. Discussion of the subject extends our understanding of Monsieur Vingtras personally as product of the system, whilst demonstrating the reasons for Jacques's revolt.

The dedication of *Le Bachelier* pinpoints a central issue, the irrelevance of the staple diet of classical literature to the needs of nineteenth-century industrial society. The subject is broached already in *L'Enfant* (see Chapter XX 'Mes Humanités'), where Jacques's classical studies are the subject of sheer pantomime. They in no way enhance his cultural awareness or aesthetic sensitivity, as is evident from his boredom when Matoussaint takes him to museums on rainy Sundays (p.337). At the same time subjects of obvious relevance are undervalued. Jacques observes, 'On a l'air d'établir qu'être fort en mathématiques c'est bon pour ceux qui n'ont rien *là*' (p.312). He himself is weak at maths, but only because of inappropriate teaching. After practical demonstrations from an Italian exile, instead of the usual abstractions and theory, he comes first in geometry (p.315).

Indeed, uninspired pedantic teaching methods are constantly under attack. Lessons are dictated and memorized with no opportunity for critical dialogue. Pupils are not encouraged to use their imagination or cultivate originality. Jacques is reproached by Legnagna for this: 'Il ne faut pas mettre du *vôtre*, je vous dis: il faut imiter les anciens' (p.331). It is when he pieces together extracts from the classics and composes his homework by what he considers to be fraudulent means, 'par le retapage et le ressemelage, par le mensonge et le vol', that he receives his master's praise and is reassured, 'Vous n'êtes au collège que pour cela, pour mâcher et remâcher ce qui a été mâché par les autres' (p.309). Disgust is apparent in Vallès's choice of imagery. Rather than developing the intellect and extending horizons, this is a degrading and futile process. Success is judged purely in terms of examination achievement. Hence the importance attached to the annual prize-giving (pp.78-83), but the clear message of the trilogy is that the academic accolade is a worthless distinction.

Moreover, the consequences of academic study may be positively harmful. Jacques mocks the flowery language of a master who insists that he model his style on Boileau (p.342). He ridicules the Latin teacher who attempts to be learned and eloquent even when giving the most mundane instruction: 'Ne portez pas vos extrémités digitales à vos cothurnes' (p.305). We laugh at such pompous latinisms, implicitly acknowledging Jacques's criticism, that the cultivation of artificial polished language distorts natural expression and stifles spontaneity. He is reproached for expressing himself simply. In his schoolmaster's words '... c'est un garçon qui aimera toujours mieux écrire "fusil" qu'*arme qui vomit la mort*' (p.342), and why not? He is drilled for so long in juggling with Latin constructions that in *Le Bachelier* we find him resorting to Latin when trying to compose a letter: 'Si je faisais d'abord ma lettre en latin? Je *pense* bien mieux en latin. Je traduirai après' (2, p.382). Vallès's irony is pointed. This is yet another distorting, inhibiting influence in Jacques's childhood.

It is the study of philosophy, however, which comes in for most criticism. In 1864 Vallès wrote 'je suis l'ennemi des philosophes' (*1*, p.436). In *L'Enfant* philosophy teachers are the prime subjects of ridicule. First of all there is the farcical scene where the self-important Beliben demonstrates his proof of the existence of God in unconvincing manner with the aid of beans, matches and assorted odds and ends (pp.68-69). Similar comic disparity pervades the presentation of Bergougnard. Although he declares, 'Je suis la Raison froide, glacée, implacable' (p.296), local people consider him a madman, and he and his household are described in a series of paradoxes (pp.298-99), not the least of which is his argument that he beats his children unrelentingly in the interests of humanity! Repeatedly the distance between the abstractions of philosophers and everyday reality is exploited to comic effect (e.g. pp.383-84), and it is no accident that it is a ludicrous difference of opinion between philosophers which is responsible for Jacques's failure at the *baccalauréat* (pp.386-90).

Vallès himself failed his *bac* four times before succeeding finally in April 1852. Even then there are suggestions that Edmond Arnould, the father of a friend and lecturer at the Sorbonne, intervened on his behalf. It has often been claimed, particularly in the aftermath of the Commune, that Vallès's criticisms of the education system were a petty reaction against a process which had branded him a failure.[4] Yet he had excelled in Greek and Latin at a time when this was considered the ultimate achievement. His setbacks were due rather to lack of application. His interest in education was not a matter of mere pique, but was deeply rooted in childhood suffering so intense that after visiting Le Puy in 1884 Vallès admitted that this was the first time he had dared approach the school buildings, the scene of so much trauma. Hence the importance he attached to the education of the young, as is clear in an article in *Le Citoyen de Paris*, 22 February 1881: 'L'Education de l'enfant! — Ah tout

[4] See Narcisse Blanpain, *Les Insurgés du 18 mars. Jules Vallès, membre de la Commune* (Paris, Lachaud, 1871), pp.24-25; Paul Bourget, 'Chronique. Psychologie d'un révolutionnaire', *Le Parlement* (19 May 1881); and Ferdinand Brunetière, 'La confession d'un réfractaire', *Revue des Deux Mondes* (1 March 1885), pp.212-24.

dépend de là; l'honneur et le bonheur! La vie des nations et la vie des hommes, la santé du monde!' This is reflected in the space accorded to the theme in the trilogy, but a novel is not the place for explicit discussion of educational issues. One has to turn to Vallès's newspaper articles for his constructive criticism, his insistence on the potential of the individual's innate curiosity, and the importance of freedom and creativity as opposed to pedantry and dogmatism. Nonetheless fundamental weaknesses are identified in L'Enfant, in so far as they become the butt of Jacques's mockery, and the direction of change is indicated. Indeed, Jacques's ideals prefigure changes which have actually taken place over the last century. Today we are sympathetic to his criticisms and find his views progressive.

Returning now to father and son, towards the end of the novel Monsieur Vingtras so resents Jacques's academic failure that he cannot bring himself to talk to him, even when he suspects he is close to suicide. Ironically it is the uneducated Madame Vingtras who acts as go-between, whilst those who have devoted years of their lives to linguistic study are incapable of simple communication. Eventually Monsieur Vingtras, insistent on being informed of his sons's intentions, is reduced to demanding a written response. Jacques produces a blunt statement: 'JE VEUX ETRE OUVRIER' (p.396). He is tired of middle-class pretensions, arid learning and indignity. To his father this is not only a disappointment of his ambitions and a challenge to his authority, but a rejection of him personally. The provocation leads to violent conflicts which are only resolved by the duel Jacques fights to defend his father's honour (pp.402-05). Monsieur Vingtras is mortified. He longs to be reunited with Jacques, but cannot swallow his pride. In the course of the novel we have seen that rigorous discipline, even Turfin's brutal severity (pp.192, 195), is part of the school routine. Monsieur Vingtras is so hardened that simple sincerity and intimacy are alien to him. He is paralysed by inhibition, a pathetic indictment of the teaching profession which he himself now recognizes as culpable: 'C'est le professorat, je te dis!...' (p.407). A broken man, he turns to his wife to act on his behalf. This meek self-effacement is the final step in his degradation, a despairing abdication of his parental role. This is underlined by the arrival of the police to arrest Jacques on his instigation. Mutual admission of guilt and failure might have led to reconciliation. The tragedy is that Monsieur Vingtras is unable openly to express his love for his son. Jacques overhears his father's confession through the bedroom wall, and his mother explains the situation to him. 'Ah! je crois qu'on eût mieux fait de m'aimer tout haut!' he sighs (p.408). Although father and son are brought closer together in spirit, physical separation becomes a necessity. The title of the chapter is 'La Délivrance'. Jacques can now leave home, freed of guilt and obligation. There is a sense of release, a feeling of hope for the future. In time, *Le Bachelier* will demonstrate that the situation is not radically transformed. Monsieur Vingtras cannot relinquish control so readily, nor can Jacques throw off his past. Nonetheless it is clear we have come to the end of a phase in their relationship.

4. Victims Together

Vallès's aim in *L'Enfant* is to defend a specific cause, 'la liberté de l'enfant' (*4*, p.282). He even talks in terms of vengeance, describing himself to Arnould as 'ton ami qui venge L'ENFANT MEURTRI' (*4*, p.289). The novel is but one step in a campaign he continues to wage in the 1880s after his return to France: 'Mon livre peut devenir le point de départ d'une campagne en faveur des petits êtres ridiculisés ou meurtris' (*4*, p.282). Small wonder then that the novel provoked shock and hostility, and that attempts were made to censor and even suppress it, after the first instalment appeared in the newspaper *Le Siècle* in 1878. Attacks on the family alienated the bourgeois. Vallès, however, was trying to focus attention on a general problem, not to settle a personal score.

Unlike much of his writing during the Second Empire, which was characterized by unalloyed bitterness, *L'Enfant* is a product of exile and nostalgic recollection of life in France. Criticism is moderated by the spirit of forgiveness, the spirit of the impending amnesty. This is not true of *L'Insurgé*, a political apology published after Vallès's return to France, and containing harsh portraits of his opponents, which show little respect for personal sensibilities. *L'Enfant* and *Le Bachelier* in contrast are marked by an ebullient sense of humour. Although Jacques never minces his words, he shows compassion not contempt for his oppressors, particularly in the closing pages of the novel.

In 1878, in strong contrast to public reaction, Vallès's close friend Arnould expressed surprise that he had so disguised and diluted his personal revolt against his parents. Factual evidence confirms that Vallès played down his parents' cruelty out of loyalty. His reply to Arnould reveals that he was also governed by artistic considerations, and the desire to exercise an influence which vindictive personal accusation would have undermined:

'Je crois que je ne devais pas dicter la colère, souligner le droit d'insurrection filiale, et que je toucherai plus sûrement ma cible pour n'avoir pas fait de moulinets avec mon fusil. C'est le lecteur qui, je l'espère, criera ce que je n'ai pas crié!' (*4*, p.250). His desire not to labour his point, but present the situation in a relatively open manner, reflects a long-held view that realism is necessarily revolutionary, irrespective of explicitly declared intentions (see *8*, pp.382-90). He wanted to expose inherent weaknesses in society, in this case in contemporary views on the exercise of authority within the home, rather than blame particular individuals. Writing to Arnould about the latter's own work in May 1877, the year before first publication of the text, Vallès observes,

> Tu sais si je suis ennemi de la guillotine paternelle, du fouet de la famille, du despotisme infâme du foyer, mais je hais l'Etat avant tout. C'est même l'Etat qui fait les pères féroces en sanctifiant l'autorité, en mettant au-dessus des têtes d'enfants comme des têtes d'insurgés un droit providentiel, une religion indiscutée, — le respect de père en fils du respect de la loi! (*4*, p.184)

The suggestion is that although the child is victim of his parents' abuse, they too are victims of conformist conditioning, and the law which condones their tyranny. This statement is not related to *L'Enfant* specifically. Yet interpretation of the text in the light of this passage may help to explain why it was perceived as so threatening, in that the challenge thus extends far beyond the justification of parents' behaviour within the home, and questions the authority of the State itself. Is such an interpretation justified? Can Jacques's parents be seen as victims for whom we feel sympathy? Also to what extent is Vallès successful in elevating the novel to more general significance than that of a personal vendetta?

Although Monsieur and Madame Vingtras are fundamentally conservative and seek to please those in power without questioning the legitimacy of their authority, Jacques portrays them nonetheless as victims of the State, in particular the

University, which requires subservience of them. Monsieur
Vingtras is also victim of his wife's domineering behaviour and
general ineptitude, which can in turn be attributed to her
anxiousness to please, coupled with inadequate social know-
how. Indeed ultimately all the family's suffering can be traced
back to their social disorientation following Monsieur Vingtras's
education and the decision to become a teacher. This is clearly
how Jacques perceives the situation. In *Le Bachelier* on his
father's death, he imagines wistfully how happy they might
otherwise have been: 'J'aurais été un beau paysan! Nous nous
serions bien aimés tous les trois, le père, la mère et le garçon!' (*2*,
p.436). Wishful thinking perhaps, but it was a view which Vallès
reiterated word for word in *Le Candidat des pauvres* (*7*, p.130).
Admittedly he goes on in this case to remark that apparently
peasants are sometimes unhappy, they can be harsh and selfish,
and their life on the land unrewarding (*7*, p.143) but *L'Enfant*
never admits of this possibility. The family's common suffering
is seen to stem from their leaving the land and so becoming
'déracinés', 'déclassés'.

The name Jacques itself, traditional nickname of the French
peasant, defines young Vingtras's peasant identity, and by
association with the term 'jacquerie' suggests his inevitable
revolt against threats to this status. His mother's attempts to disguise his origins under a façade of social graces are doomed to
failure (p.281). When he cries out deliriously at the headmaster's
party, 'Nanette! Nanette!' (p.283), this is his suppressed peasant
identity reasserting itself despite all. Even the determined
Madame Vingtras cannot turn her back on her past, and takes a
defensive pride in local singing, dancing and accent, despite her
pretensions. She may try to be genteel, yet by nature she is blunt,
and lets the side down frequently.

The farcical scenes during the family's journeys from one
town to another demonstrate forcefully the effects of their social
and geographical uprooting. It is here that they are at their most
pathetic and inept. In Saint-Etienne, Orléans and Nantes in
turn, they find themselves lost and insecure, in the dark and
cold. Jacques observes ruefully, 'Notre spécialité est d'en-
combrer de notre présence et de gêner de nos bagages la vie

des cités où nous pénétrons' (pp.262-63). They do not know their place in society. Self-importance does not command respect; it is Madame Vingtras's meanness that attracts attention. The family sit blocking the pavement, 'seuls comme un paquet d'orphelins' (p.243) — a comment which emphasizes the cause, the break with family ties and traditions. Yet the common experience of ridicule and alienation has its compensations in bringing all three together and eliciting the reader's sympathy for parents and child alike.

Indeed from the outset it is clear that in so far as Jacques attributes the family plight to the problem of social identity, he attributes it to mistaken ambition and not malevolence on his parents' part. Often he puts himself in their place, even if only to ridicule his mother's logic or justify his father's disappointment in him, tongue-in-cheek: 'On est un insolent vis-à-vis de son père, quand on pense qu'avec la *toge* on est pauvre, qu'avec le tablier de cuir on est libre! C'est moi qui ai tort, il a raison de me battre' (p.197). Such passages subvert the view they ostensibly defend. Yet the view is not in itself unreasonable, for it is instinct and personality which motivate Jacques's rejection of his father's priorities rather than logic. The balance of sympathy is not entirely in Jacques's favour.

The vicissitudes of personal relationships within the family also mellow the presentation of both parents. I have discussed the impact of Monsieur Vingtras's adultery on his relations with Jacques. The effects on Madame Vingtras are more traumatic still. Her marriage and status are threatened, her confidence destroyed, with the result that, by the time she visits Jacques in Paris, she is much readier to accept his independence. When Jacques blurts out his resentment at the suffering she has caused him, and admits he wants to be free of his parents, the effect is dramatic. All pretence and hypocrisy is swept away, and for the first time mother and son confront one another honestly. Madame Vingtras, pale and weeping, is completely transfigured in Jacques's eyes: 'Quand elle releva son visage, je ne la reconnaissais plus: il y avait sur ce masque de paysanne toute la poésie de la douleur; elle était blanche comme une grande dame, avec des larmes comme des perles dans les yeux' (pp.367-68).

Ironically, only now does she acquire the grandeur and status she has so long sought. Both mother and child are sincerely ashamed and repentant. Following this scene, in a symbolic gesture which gives the measure of her transformation, Madame Vingtras hands over her purse to Jacques. Her ambitions and illusions shattered first by her husband and now her son, she becomes utterly self-effacing, giving way to both men, whilst trying to keep the peace between them. Jacques now refers to her as 'Ma pauvre mère' (p.391) or 'La pauvre femme' (p.395), and feels for her in this unhappy role.

The interaction between parents and child then goes beyond a simple movement from repression to revolt, for when revolt surfaces in open confrontation, this leads in turn to reconciliation. The same progression can be traced in relationships between mother and child, father and son, although in the latter case the reconciliation remains tacit. This nuances considerably the initial contrast between oppressor and oppressed. As his parents' confidence ebbs, so Jacques increasingly asserts his identity and erodes their domination. His parents' marriage, 'ce mariage de la débine et de la misère' (p.44), is evidently far from happy, whatever the reasons, and by the end of the novel we are bound to pity father and mother rather than condemn. They are left together bitterly disillusioned, while Jacques has at least the hope of forging a new life. Since he has come into contact with journalists and political activists in Paris, and has studied the history of the Revolution, his thoughts have moved to another plane. He does not want to harbour personal grudges, and longs for a more glorious role: 'On n'était plus fouetté par sa mère, ni par son père, on était fusillé par l'ennemi, et l'on mourait comme Bara' (p.371). He now identifies his personal rebellion with the broader revolutionary struggles which mark nineteenth-century French political history. Vallès thus points the way ahead to the conflicts of *Le Bachelier* and *L'Insurgé*, while underlining his broader theme of social disorientation and disintegration.

Jacques's personality is also crucial to the overall balance of sympathy. He is more attractive than his parents, with his sense of humour, his generosity, his readiness to sacrifice himself, and finally his forgiveness. Yet he is far from becoming a child martyr. He emerges as too robust and sure of his instinctive leanings to succumb to family pressures. The theme of aggressive retaliation marks the beginning and end of the novel, with the bite of the suckling baby in the opening paragraph, and the duel of the final chapter. Numerous episodes illustrate Jacques's masochism and powers of endurance. We are also repeatedly reminded that we are witnessing the childhood of a Communard in the making, as Jacques looks ahead, declaring: 'Ma vie sera une vie de bataille. C'est le sort de celles qui commencent comme cela. Je le sens bien' (p.401). Unlike Ernest Pitou, for Jacques suicide never constitutes a genuine danger, whatever his father's fears (p.395) or his own fleeting temptations (p.401). He is emotionally and physically scarred, but suffering kindles the spirit of combat. When *Le Testament d'un blagueur* was published in 1869, Vallès was not to know how fundamentally the following two years of French political history would change the pattern of his life. After 1871 he sees and reflects his childhood in a new light, and it becomes essential to portray Jacques as a resilient child and future insurrectionist.

Jacques's situation could also be much worse, as comparisons with Vallès's own experience confirm. He has sympathetic friends and relatives, and even his parents have compensating qualities. Madame Vingtras's sheer zeal and vivacity in oppression are appealing. Also, she and her husband so rarely see eye to eye that it is only for the briefest of spells that they join forces against Jacques. It is of comfort to him too that he is not alone in his suffering. Companions in misery figure throughout the novel, setting his experiences in perspective, and allowing Vallès to suggest the universality of the problems he raises. In a highly selective sketch of childhood in Le Puy, Jacques recalls prisoners being marched past in handcuffs, looking ill and despairing rather than wicked (p.42). On passing the coach-station he is reminded of a pale young lady waiting presumably for her lover for days on end, before losing hope and drowning herself (pp.91-92). On market day he feels pity for a vagrant, 'fils d'un guillotiné ou d'un galérien', a down-and-out with a shady past (pp.114-15). Whatever the scene, the image of the sympathetic victim recurs.

Within this broad theme of compassion for the oppressed, there are specific examples of children who are beaten as severely as Jacques, and long to leave home, like Ricard the bed-wetter (pp.203-05) or Vidaljan, the 'sorcerer's apprentice' (pp.205-08). Madame Vingtras herself has other victims, like Jacques's cousin Marianne (pp.234-38).

Two figures in particular, however, extend the study of child-hood suffering, namely Mademoiselle Miolan and Louisette Bergougnard. Although the former is a twenty-year-old, dying of a broken heart, she is entirely dependent on Monsieur and Madame Brignolin, who treat her as one of their children. Sig-nificantly both figures are female, for this accentuates the impression of delicacy and vulnerability, but their situations are set in sharp contrast. Mademoiselle Miolan is in poor shape physically, but the family dote on her. She may not be able to forget her grief, but she responds to their attention, and is happy to see those around her enjoying themselves (pp.211-15). Bergougnard, on the other hand, tortures his children merci-lessly (p.298). As a result his son Bonaventure becomes a repulsive sadist. Louisette is spared so long as she lives with an aunt, but when the latter dies, she returns to her parents, a rosy, gay child, only to be convulsed with terror and driven to dis-traction by her father's attacks. Ultimately she dies as much from emotional as physical distress: 'Elle mourut de douleur à dix ans' (p.301). The parallel with Mademoiselle Miolan's situation lends greater plausibility to the notion of death from a broken heart, whilst accentuating the contrast between the healing power of love and affection and the outrageousness of Bergougnard's cold-blooded cruelty.

Jacques is more emotional and outspoken in this episode than at any other point in the novel. Monsieur and Madame Vingtras are not exempt from blame. They have already demonstrated their callousness in ridiculing Jacques's sentimentality after the death of the dog Myrza, when they force Jacques to dump her body in the rubbish (pp.239-40). Their insensitivity is revealed again when Madame Vingtras jealously snatches Louisette's scarf from Jacques, and then goes on to destroy Marguerite's bouquet (pp.303-04). Jacques's parents stand idly by, allowing events to take their course, even upholding Bergougnard's authority, and reproaching Louisette for displeasing him (p.303). Society at large is similarly accused of condoning absolute parental authority and allowing Bergougnard's actions to go unpunished: 'Et on ne l'a pas guillotiné, ce père-là! On ne lui a pas appliqué la peine du talion à cet assassin de son enfant, on n'a pas supplicié ce lâche, on ne l'a pas enterré vivant à côté de la morte!' (pp.301-02). This is the crux of Jacques's and Vallès's indignation, that in such instances the law condones what is tantamount to murder.

The power which the law grants parents over their children is taken up again when Monsieur Vingtras threatens to have Jacques arrested if he sets off to Paris without his permission. He even has his copy of *Le Code* in front of him to indicate the clauses setting out his authority (p.391). Louis Vallez had exercised this power over his son to have him interned in an asylum, and Jules was horrified not only by the experience itself but also by the fact that such acts were legal. Jacques feels he has done nothing wrong (p.401), and yet his father has the power to have him sent to prison because of a personal disagreement. He asserts his determination to fight to remedy this situation:

> Je défendrai les DROITS DE L'ENFANT, comme d'autres les DROITS DE L'HOMME.
>
> Je demanderai si les pères ont liberté de vie et de mort sur le corps et l'âme de leurs fils; si Monsieur Vingtras a le droit de me martyriser parce que j'ai eu peur d'un métier de misère, et si Monsieur Bergougnard peut encore crever la poitrine d'une Louisette. (pp.401-022)

This particular cause is not pursued in subsequent volumes of the trilogy, but it is a campaign which Vallès fights vigorously in his journalism of the 1880s. In *Le Réveil*, 9 January 1882, he demands a reform of legislation: 'L'enfant est à la merci des parents bêtes ou féroces, de ceux qui l'ont engendré ou de ceux qui l'élèvent, et il faudra que le Code soit déchiré pour que cela change'. He even proposes a League for the Protection of the

Rights of the Child, which was actually founded at a meeting in the offices of *Le Réveil* on 22 January 1882, although no concrete measures appear to have resulted. Nonetheless, when cases of child abuse appeared before the courts, Vallès took the opportunity to express his views, and continued to attract attention to the issue.

His feelings on the matter were strong, even though at times Jacques minimizes the sense of outrage, and appears to defend his parents: 'Mon père et ma mère me battent, mais eux seuls dans le monde ont le droit de me frapper' (p.195). In this instance.he has been describing how deeply hurt he was when his teacher Turfin hit him, so hurt that he recalls the incident with intense hatred when he meets Turfin in the streets of Paris years later (2, pp.392-95). The point he is making is that Turfin's blow is a contemptuous and gratuitous demonstration of superiority, whereas parental blows are an integral part of a highly complex relationship, and as such can be more readily justified. He has come to accept such treatment from his parents, although the final chapters of the novel demonstrate his belief that he should not have had to. The distinction is crucial. Yet it is not so much Monsieur and Madame Vingtras individually who are accused. The State and society at large are ultimately responsible.

The intentional omission of the more shocking aspects of Vallès's own experience, or their transfer to another household, the degree of sympathy shown for Monsieur and Madame Vingtras's plight and the explicit attack on *Le Code*, all confirm that *L'Enfant* goes beyond autobiography to become a novel inspired by personal experience of childhood, yet assuming much broader significance. Much has changed over the past century. In Western society children are often entitled to their own legal representation. They can be made wards of court or taken into the care of a local authority, precisely in order to protect their rights. Certainly their wishes are respected very much more than a century ago. However, the reconciliation of a child's inevitable dependence with respect for his or her basic liberties will always remain a problem. So too the question of authority, for today there are those who challenge the right of the State to assume the traditional responsibilities of the parent, and given his hatred of the State, one suspects that Vallès, were he alive, might well be amongst them.

5. Style, Perspective and Form

No study of *L'Enfant* would be complete without some consideration of style and form, as both reflect the desire for freedom and individual expression which emerges in the discussion of themes, and demonstrate Vallès's search for a new form of literature. In *L'Enfant* we see Jacques's lack of interest in classical literature (p.311) and celebrated French writers (pp.397-98). In subsequent volumes his disrespect for the literary establishment becomes more apparent still, and in *L'Insurgé* he boasts that in his writing he is breaking new ground:

> Je n'ai pas regardé, comme on l'enseigne à la Sorbonne, si ce que j'écrivais ressemblait à du Pascal ou à du Marmontel, à du Juvénal ou à du Paul-Louis Courier, à Saint-Simon ou à Sainte-Beuve, je n'ai eu ni le respect des tropes, ni la peur des néologismes ... (*3*, p.65)

At this stage in the trilogy the distance between Vingtras and Vallès is little more than a convention, and the text of *L'Enfant* can usefully be examined in the light of such claims. It is indeed marked by bold innovation, appropriately combined with other distinctive features of childhood: blunt simplicity, terrific energy and an irrepressible sense of humour.

Style

In the place of smooth conventional literary periods we find rapid series of short simple phrases, constantly interrupting the flow of language, as in the breathless rhythms of Jacques's ecstatic exclamations: 'Je suis grand, je vais à l'école. Oh! la belle petite école! Oh! la belle rue! et si vivante, les jours de foire' (p.47). This is a feature characteristic of dialogue, which figures frequently but, as in this particular case, not only dialogue, but the first person narrative too has the emotional rhythms, the directness, intimacy and informality of the spoken word. Utterances trail off into nothingness, or are completed by actions or gestures. In a letter to Emile Gautier (published in *Les Belles Lectures* in June 1952), talking of his style in letter-writing, Vallès comments, 'je tiens une conversation et je fais des gestes plutôt que je n'écris'. The remark is equally applicable to the trilogy, and dashes, dots, italics, capitals and exclamation marks indicate rhythm, emphasis and intonation.

The narrator's approach is childlike, analogical rather than analytical. Facts and actions are simply stated without complex whys and wherefores, and complex nominalization is avoided by the use of numerous simple phrases. A contemporary of Vallès, Maurice Barrès, writing in the newspaper *Le Voltaire*, 11 June 1886, characterized Vallès's style as 'une manière formée par simplification, par diminution successive'. In 1930 Christiane Delforge, in her comparison of the different versions of *L'Enfant* published during Vallès's lifetime, also traced a trend towards simplification. She noted the systematic shortening of sentences through the replacement of relative clauses by phrases in opposition, infinitives and complements by single adjectives, verbal expressions by single nouns etc. There was a conscious move to concision and simple syntax on Vallès's part. Originally complex sentences are broken up. Simple juxtaposition replaces logical subordination, producing a more primitive sentence with a staccato rhythm.

Syntactical norms go by the board and, in keeping with the oral quality, we find familiar language like the following: 'Comme j'attends après lui!' (p.56) and 'Ce n'était pas pour de rire, du tout' (p.57). Vallès was not the first to introduce ordinary speech in his novels. Hugo, Balzac and Eugène Sue had set the trend, but Vallès, like Zola, was a pioneer in reproducing it in narrative and dialogue alike. Familiar speech is often characterized by ellipsis as in the expression: 'les buveurs faisaient tapage' (p.63). In *L'Enfant* this is symptomatic of a movement towards economy at every level. Sentences often have no finite verbs, the copulas 'avoir' and 'être' being most commonly omitted, as in this portrait of Aunt Marion's husband: 'Un beau laboureur blond, cinq pieds sept pouces, pas de barbe, mais des poils qui luisent sur son cou, un cou rond, gras, doré ...' (p.50). Description is reduced to disjointed shorthand notation of significant detail in a telegraphic style.

Where others resort to lengthy paraphrase, Vallès blithely coins a new word. The neologisms Jacques mentions (see above, p.60) appear with increasing frequency in the trilogy.[5] In L'Enfant the following pejorative terms are coined to convey Jacques's contempt for schoolwork and the teaching profession: 'bachellerie', 'latinage' (p.55); 'pionnage' (p.251); 'latinasserie' and 'grécaillerie' (p.290). He describes eating a fertilized egg as a crime: '*coquicide*' (p.53). A neologism conveys enthusiasm and intimacy when talking about his favourite author of sea-faring adventure-stories, 'mon *tempêtard* favori' (p.241). He demonstrates lack of constraint in irreverent experimentation with language.

This is evident too when he seeks to convey sounds. Rather than engaging in lengthy description, he devises a form of phonetic notation, recreating quality and rhythm in onomatopoeic expressions. There are the insistent resounding noises of Madame Vingtras beating Jacques: 'Vlin! Vlan! Zon! Zon!' (p.39), or the low and high notes of Madame Brignolin at the piano: '*Boum, boum, hi, hi!*' (p.209). Vallès notes the noise and movement of a horse trotting along: 'La bête va l'amble ta ta ta, ta ta ta!' (p.60), and the comic sounds of Jacques reciting Greek with the cold induced by his mother's efforts to clear his nose: '*Benin, aeïde! — atchiou! theia Beleiadeo, — atchiou!* Je traîne dans le ridicule le vieil *Hobère!*' (p.311). Rather than cultivating style as an aim in itself, Vallès is resourceful in his adaptation of language to his own ends, innovating to humorous effect, with childlike playfulness and lack of sophistication.

Puns are an excellent illustration. Jacques's intrepid attitude to tropes (see above, p.60) is apparent throughout the trilogy, above all in Le Bachelier where they are all the more in keeping as he earns his living by collecting puns (2, pp.346-47). Also Vallès is parodying here the battles of wit of student days, and

---

[5] See B. Nikolov (*18*) for a detailed study of neologisms in Vallès's writing.

indulges in excruciating wordplay. In *L'Enfant*, the com-
paratively small number of puns is equally appropriate to the
firm rooting of the context in immediate concrete reality.
Jacques interrupts the painful silence which follows the family's
arrival in Saint-Etienne by breaking a glass picture-frame, and is
delighted 'd'avoir dérangé ce silence, *cassé la glace*' (p.125).
Monsieur Brignolin, a chemist, is also his wife's cuckold: 'il est
toujours dans les *cornues*' (pp.210-11). Loud laughter not subtle
nuance is Vallès's aim, and lest the reader be slow to perceive the
duality, key words are underlined.

Puns are devices of economy, features of an elliptical style. So
too are zeugmas like the following: 'Je me rejette dans le livre ...
et je le dévore — avec un peu de thon, des larmes de cognac —
devant la flamme de la cheminée' (p.146). Vallès derives bizarre
effects from incongruous intermingling of the literal and metaphorical: 'Ma mère a toujours la main sur le gigot et un pied
dans la tombe à propos de cette bonne' (p.276), or the abstract
and the concrete: 'L'autorité veille dans le corsage de la bonne
comme dans la culotte de l'enfant' (p.275). Here the combination of ellipsis and free movement between different levels of
reference leads to particularly cryptic lines which can only be
decoded in context, but there are less elusive instances, for
example when the Vingtras family learns that the headmaster
does not approve of corporal punishment, and Jacques
comments wryly, 'La nouvelle est arrivée aux oreilles de mon
père et a protégé les miennes' (p.269).

The effect is to shock and disconcert, as do the symmetrical
patterns of balance and antithesis found, for example, in the
neat chiasmus-figure: 'ma jeunesse s'éveille, ma mère dort ...
Ma jeunesse s'éteint, ma mère est éveillée!' (p.253). Vallès revels
in apparently paradoxical statements, for example when the
paragraph introducing the highly vivacious but deaf and dumb
Aunt Amélie culminates in the assertion: 'rien n'est bavard
comme un sourd-muet' (p.50). Instead of proceeding in a
smooth reassuring flow, the language itself, with its abrupt
rhythms and contrasts, disrupts our thoughts and prompts
deeper reflection. Wordplay is a feature of childhood.[6] It is a

6 See W.D. Redfern (*34*, *35*) for further discussion of wordplay.

source of amusement. It is also a symbol and instrument of revolt, the simultaneous revolt of Jacques the child and Vallès the writer.

Vallès's early journalism, in which he repeatedly reworked a few pet themes, has on occasion led to his being accused of exploiting a limited vocabulary,[7] but in *L'Enfant* it would be more appropriate to talk of logorrhoea, as Jacques recalls his mother's blows: 'elle m'a travaillé dans tous les sens, pincé, balafré, tamponné, bourré, souffleté, frotté, cardé et tanné ...' (p.216). The accumulation of *-er* verbs itself conveys the impression of relentless battering, and Jacques's resourcefulness matches his mother's, as he finds verb after verb to enrich and vary this central impression. His inventive repetition is a source of humour and vitality, definitely not a sign of weakness. Delforge's study (*16*, pp.11-19) underlines the colourfulness of the final version of *L'Enfant*. Neutral terms are replaced by emotive expressions: the verb 'piocher' is inserted in the line '*faisant* mes devoirs' (p.64), 'mourir' in 'Je regarde *s'en aller* la nuit' (p.225), 'voler' in 'ils me *prennent* ce bout de soie ...' (p.303). Vallès's talent lies in exploiting everyday language to the full, and nowhere more so than in his mastery of sound and rhythm. A passage describing Jacques's enjoyment of working-class company well illustrates this point: 'Ernest, Charles ou Barnabé, un Vincent ou un Fabre, m'appelait pour une glissade, une promenade ou une bourrade, à propos de bottes ou de marmelade; il y avait toujours quelque tonneau, quelque baquet, quelque querelle ou quelque pot à vider pour aider la boutique ou l'échoppe, le travail ou la rigolade' (p.133). Accumulation, repetition, assonance and rhythm convey incessant variety, energy and industry. The correspondence between ideas and expression is particularly evident here. Look too at the long paragraph conveying Aunt Amélie's extra-ordinary gossiping (extraordinary given that she is dumb), which pauses only once at a full-stop. The lines are broken down into short insistent sequences which all contribute to the impression of effervescent vitality (p.50).

[7] For details see Pamela M. Moores, *Jules Vallès and the Social Role of Literature* (Ph.D. Thesis, University of Leicester, 1977), pp.222-24.

Defiance of convention also determines our angle of vision. We find Jacques examining his grandmother's curtains with his head between his legs, in order to see what shapes he can identify in the pattern (p.53). On many occasions relatively normal situations are presented in an unusual perspective. Evoking an incident when he almost bumps into a waiter in a restaurant, Jacques tells us: 'Il m'arrive deux ou trois fois de m'opposer absolument au passage d'une sole et d'un œuf sur le plat' (p.360). The situation itself is potentially farcical, as he tries desperately to avoid the waiter, who is piled high with dishes. However, the comedy is underlined by the depersonalized manner in which he describes the incident. The waiter is not even mentioned! Vallès delights in defying normal constraints, animating the inanimate and dehumanizing the human. Frequently he dissociates parts of the body from the individuals to whom they belong, as in the comic lines: 'On a amené cette bosse chez le proviseur' (p.97), and 'Il nous vient beaucoup d'estomac à la maison' (p.278). The effect is bizarre, but not unusual in a world where Jacques himself experiences the sensation of being detached from parts of his body, after his mother's thorough cleansing of his nose (pp.310-11).

Imagery likewise suggests odd parallels. Jacques compares his own awkward gait to the movement of 'un ressort rouillé qui se déroule mal' (p.106) or, collapsing under the weight of a pile of luggage, and wondering helplessly which way to go, he says he looks like 'un télescope qu'on ferme' (p.244). Although hilariously apt, these are not the first parallels which spring to mind! On describing great Aunt Agnès Vallès selects grotesque detail:

> ... la barbe grise, un bouquet de poils ici, une petite mèche qui frisotte par là, et de tous côtés des poireaux comme des groseilles, qui ont l'air de bouillir sur sa figure.
> Pour mieux dire, sa tête rappelle, par le haut, à cause du serre-tête noir, une pomme de terre brûlée et, par le bas, une pomme de terre germée ... (p.51)

Everyday objects become the basis for bold and striking comparisons. In their studies of Vallès's imagery, Delforge (*16*), Dubois[8] and Giaufret Colombani (*18*) alike demonstrate his exploitation of familiar realms of experience. He uses 'images internes', stemming naturally from the context they describe. In *L'Enfant* the rustic scene and domestic environment, and images of plant and animal life, especially circus animals, are prominent. Yet the familiarity of referents does not impair effectiveness or originality, which depend upon the parallel established, as demonstrated by the example quoted above, where the reference to leeks, redcurrants and potatoes conveys the unexpected irreverent insights of childhood. Elsewhere a central theme is underlined as Vallès, in his description of the peasants, talks of 'leurs sabots qui ont l'air de souches, où se sont enfoncés leurs pieds' and 'la peau comme de l'écorce, et des veines comme des racines d'arbres' (p.93). Simple local analogies reinforce the theme of harmony with nature, and the impression of immutable security. Images here are not abstruse or highly imaginative poetic creations. They are simple but pointed.

So too is the use of colour. Jacques contrasts the feminine pinks of Madame Brignolin (p.218) and the deputy-head's wife (p.272), and his mother's fetish for shades of green and yellow (pp.76, 79-81, 218, 272). More importantly, however, here again we trace a parallelism with developments at the thematic level. In an article in *La Constitution*, 25 March 1872, Vallès associates primary colours with a childlike lack of sophistication, and links the gaudy colours of London with the infantile lack of politicization of the British population. In *L'Enfant* Jacques remarks, 'Tout ce qui avait des tons vifs ou des couleurs fauves, gros comme un pois ou comme une orange, tout ce qui était une tache de couleur vigoureuse ou gaie, tout cela faisait marque dans mon œil d'enfant triste' (p.72). In the early chapters of the novel his nostalgic recollection of Le Puy and the surrounding area presents bright multicoloured sketches, and the landscape is radiant, with bubbling clear streams glistening in the sunlight (e.g. pp.67-68). In Saint-Etienne, by contrast, he

---

[8] See Jacques Dubois, *Révolte et ferveur de Jules Vallès. Etude de style* (Université de Liège, Mémoire, 1957).

notes greys and blacks and the tarnished colours of industrial and city life. The grass is now 'roussie', scorched and condemned.[9] The red is that of coke and bricks, sinister, 'rougeâtres et ternes comme des grumeaux de sang caillé' (p.212). In Nantes the river Loire is stained with black and assumes 'une couleur glauque'. Even the farmworkers' clothes are 'blanc sale' (p.268), distastefully soiled, not openly dirty. As Jacques moves from childhood innocence and rustic harmony to increasing involvement in the social conflict, pure colours are polluted, while at the same time the political associations of colour, evoked relatively lightheartedly in *L'Enfant* (pp.270-71), assume increasing importance. The jaundiced yellow and mournful grey of *Le Bachelier* give way in *L'Insurgé* to the red of bloody socialist revolution and the black of suffering and death. Bright colouring is gone, simple pleasures left behind.

This reflection of thematic progression in colour is only one aspect of the strong visual impact of the novel. Vallès had been influenced by artists like Courbet, Pilotell and André Gill who collaborated with him in producing the newspaper *La Rue* in the 1860s. His character sketches are marked by their pictorial qualities. His imagery, rather than developing subtle nuance, is often a means of visualizing ideas or situations in terms of fable-like simplicity. In Paul Bourget's eyes this is an indication of immaturity and an inability to communicate in abstract terms,[10] but in all his writing Vallès sought to avoid this. He wanted to appeal to the masses (although his frequent cultural allusions and latinisms pose problems for the less educated reader). Moreover, since his focus here is the experiences of a child, simplicity must be seen as a positive quality. When one compares the unpretentiousness of *L'Enfant* to the hyperbole and rhetoric of some of Vallès's journalism, the correspondence between subject matter and expression is bound to seem more than a happy accident. Delforge's demonstration that the impression of simple spontaneous expression is achieved only as

[9] 'Roussi' also means heretical, thus reinforcing the suggestion that nature is condemned by the progress of industry.

[10] See P. Bourget, 'Jules Vallès' in *Etudes et portraits: portraits d'écrivains et notes d'esthétique* (Paris, Librairie Plon, 1905), p.141.

a result of careful correction and improvement confirms this. Ironically Vallès's style is often deemed to be his greatest achievement, but the explanation lies in Antoine Albalat's comment on his writing: 'On peut dire que le style consiste à n'en pas avoir'[11] — a paradox which would have pleased Vallès both in its import and formulation.

Perspective

Another revolutionary feature of the novel for the period, as Philippe Lejeune argues (*21*, p.10) is the reconstitution of the child's voice in the narrative role. Childhood is seen through the eyes of the child, though not exclusively so, for the narrative is shared between Vingtras child and adult. In the opening paragraph, a retrospective adult narrator addresses the reader, but subsequently the child himself sometimes takes over. Young Jacques appears to address us directly when, after betraying his father's faults, he reproaches himself, 'oh! je vends un secret de famille!' (p.307). Yet Vallès moves so imperceptibly between adult and child that at times the child appears to benefit from the adult's insight. Points of transition are so frequent that one comes to accept a vague fusion of perspectives, and the historical dimension is eclipsed. The present is used both for storytelling and recounting current reflections. Its widespread use creates an impression of simplicity, immediacy and informality. Whereas the past tenses distance and contain events in ordered chronological and causal sequences, use of the present destroys the sense of order and control, and the reader is subjected to a stream of diverse impressions recreating rather the quality of experience. Confusion is compounded by periodic reversion to the more traditional past historic for, although in each instance justifications of its use can be found, there is no overall logic or consistency.

In dialogue, as Lejeune points out, we hear Jacques's voice rarely, in true reflection of his subordination and repression. It is the adults' opinions which are openly aired, while his view

[11] See A. Albalat, 'Jules Vallès artiste', in *L'Art d'écrire, ouvriers et procédés* (Paris, G. Havard fils, 1896), p.218.

emerges through ironic undermining of their opinions. Vallès plays on the contrast between the child's innocence and the criticism implied in the narrator's irony. Lejeune talks of 'le développement sophistiqué de la "sous conversation" au style indirect libre qui représente ce que l'enfant pense sans pouvoir le dire, en même temps que s'y reflètent les jugements de valeur de l'adulte' (*21*, p.24). This 'style indirect libre' integrates and confuses the two voices as one is mimed within the other. The same process is at work when Jacques ironically voices his mother's logic (see above, pp.21, 25) for, as Lejeune observes, 'Il s'agit d'amener l'adversaire à "se suicider avec sa propre langue" '(*21*, p.25). As time passes, the adult narrator figures less often, as the gap between the two perspectives closes and Jacques the character comments for himself. Nonetheless the disruptive ambiguity persists.

The variety and complexity of the narrative are, however, greater still than this suggests. A sample will illustrate the point. Let us examine the preparation of the prize-giving costume, from page 79: 'Jacques, je vais te faire une redingote avec ça ...' to page 80 and the words: '... ovales comme des olives et verts comme des cornichons'.

In the first half of the page we have direct speech from both mother and child, but characteristically only one short plea from the latter. The first-person narrative of Jacques the child moves between past and present tenses. But it is Madame Vingtras who is immediately responsible for most shifts of perspective as she addresses her remarks first to her child 'tu', then to Jacques the imaginary 'Monsieur', hence 'vous', and finally, talking to nobody in particular, she refers to him in the third person, remarking, 'on fera une redingote à Jacques avec ça'.

The first eight lines of the second half of the page are a typical illustration of Vallès's use of the 'style indirect libre', as Jacques talks to himself, and mimes his mother's expressions of devotion using present and future tenses. Then, unexpectedly, we move to a third person narrative equally removed from both characters: 'La mère de Jacques lui fait même kiki dans le cou'. Next the reader himself is directly addressed as 'vous', and the adult Jacques reviews his development from a distance in the third person and past historic: 'Ah! quand, plus tard, il fut dur pour les Polonais, quoi d'étonnant! Le nom de cette nation, voyez-vous, resta chez lui cousu à un souvenir terrible'. The following paragraphs introduce yet more variation, but this section alone demonstrates the volatility and indeterminate character of the narrative. One moment the narrative enacts Jacques's agony: 'Le ciel ne m'entend pas!' A moment later we are viewing him from afar. One moment he is a child, the next in his mother's shoes, and the next an adult observer. The shifts are particularly marked and frequent here, reflecting the crisis of identity which this episode provokes, but throughout the novel shifts of voice and perspective keep the reader constantly on his toes, disrupting and modifying expectations. This unpredictable, deliberately discordant narrative is yet another expression of revolt.

Finally the use of the 'style indirect libre' in this passage points to one of the most distinctive features of Vallès's style, his irony. This is an aspect of his writing he mentions frequently, for it is central to his combination of serious theme and comic presentation. He talks of 'l'arme de l'ironie' as 'un poignard à manche joli, à reflet de lame bleue, avec une petite larme blanche au bout et des taches de sang dans le fil' (5, p.116). It combines entertainment with a sharp cutting edge and the power to drive its point home ruthlessly. It also has a clear psychological motivation in the trilogy. Vallès talks of 'l'ironie qui console' (4, p.172) asserting 'Il faut rire pour n'être pas trop sombre' (4, p.231). Irony is an invaluable outlet for Jaques's repressed emotions; in Vallès's words, 'l'ironie est la soupape par où la liberté s'échappe' (1, p.1026). It is also a form of disguise and self-defence, as Jacques reveals: 'Je couvrirai éternellement mes émotions intimes du masque de l'insouciance et de la perruque de l'ironie' (2, p.26). Vallès claims he appreciates all forms of irony from the most subtle to the most barbaric (1, p.583) and categorizes L'Enfant as 'mon œuvre d'ironie joyeuse' (9, IV, p.1461). With humour as with colour, in the course of the trilogy there is a movement from energetic variety to a narrower focus of sombre intensity, although humour survives to the very end in the form of savage caricature.

In *L'Enfant* it is Jacques's youthful exuberance and the sheer variety of sources and moods of humour which give the novel such appeal. There are the farcical pantomime scenes like Antoine Vingtras's birthday, and the prizegiving. There is also a Rabelaisian touch as Jacques 'l'indécrottable' (p.325) is fascinated by soiled pants (pp.47, 96), manure (pp.108, 373), chamber-pots (p.82), latrines (pp.140, 307), constipation (p.296), purgatives (p.311), the anus (p.308) and 'le derrière' generally. He is down-to-earth with a vengeance, preferring in place of academic study 'le ruisseau de Farreyrolles, la bouse des vaches, le crottin des chevaux, et ramasser des pissenlits pour faire de la salade' (p.309). The choice of 'pissenlits' with their diarrhetic associations demonstrates Vallès's wit even in scatological passages. Jacques is an appealing storyteller precisely because, despite the pressures he is subjected to, he bounces back, restores the balance. He is critical but tolerant, saddened yet amusing. When writing about Gounod, Vallès says he likes 'les martyrs qui sont rigolos à leur moment' (9, IV, p.874). This is Jacques, summing up the blend of tender sympathy and bold hilarity his story provokes. He has no time for self-indulgent sentimentality. Even at the end of *L'Enfant*, when we witness a moving reconciliation, the emotional mood is punctured as Madame Vingtras, in typical deflating manner, exclaims, 'Une autre fois, Jacques, mets au moins ton vieux pantalon!' (p.409).

Form

Similar disruption characterizes the formal composition of novel. Yet this is in no way due to it having first been published as a serial in *Le Siècle,* for Vallès handed over a completed manuscript, which was only subsequently divided into instalments. Jacques Dubois in *Les Romanciers français de l'instantané* classifies Vallès's writing as impressionist. Amongst the features of his definition of impressionist literature we find reliance on feeling and concentration on recreating the intensity of an experience, resulting in the replacement of the traditional 'récit' by episodes in loose association. This is readily observed

in *L'Enfant*. Traditional divisions of narrative and description
are abandoned. So too are formal introductions. We plunge 'in
medias res'. In a letter presented by Léon Millot in *La Justice*, 24
February 1885, Vallès disputed the need to enumerate all the
logical links in a development: 'Je crois à peine à ces nécessités
d'enchaînement'. In *L'Enfant* we are subjected to a series of
sketches which make their impact rather by a process of accumulation. The elliptical style and rudimentary syntax create a
general impression rather than unfolding full, explicit
descriptions. The use of the spoken language too, with its short
phrases and numerous dislocations, increases the sense of fragmentation. Details are jotted down with no attempt at synthesis
and integration, baldly juxtaposed like colour on the
impressionist canvas. There is also the strong visual impact
mentioned above (p.67), characters suggested in a swift deft
outline, and more particularly the radiant scenes demonstrating
the fascination for light effects to be found in impressionist
painting. Finally, Vallès's experience in journalism had made
him particularly aware of the visual impact achieved by
attention to layout of the page, as is evident in the careful
arrangement of the dedication of each novel, so as to maximize
the impact of essential elements. In 1879, in a letter to Albert
Callet, fellow editor of *La Rue*, he stressed the importance of
aerating the text: 'Des jours, de l'air, sous forme de blancs
diviseurs ou de tirets ou d'étoiles ou de rosaces — n'importe!' In
L'Enfant he avoids offputting expanses of dense uninterrupted
prose. The text is broken up by passages of dialogue, italics,
capitals, dashes, dots and blanks. An important line stands out,
isolated physically like Jacques's cry for joy, when he finds
himself free from his mother's control:

Je suis donc libre! (p.84)

At climactic moments of unspeakable tension and emotion, the
narrative is interrupted by an entire line of dots (pp.124, 244,
303, 329, 367, 388, 407), as suspense is reproduced directly. One
might compare this to the suggestive qualities of impressionist
painting. Analogies between painting and writing remain of

necessity tenuous, but their virtue in this case is that they high-light distinctive characteristics of Vallès's writing.

His own comments confirm the aptness of the description 'impressionist' when, on introducing *Le Testament d'un blagueur*, he writes: 'Il avait déposé là ses souvenirs par tranches et miettes ... Ce sont des pages curieuses, comme toutes les pages des Mémoires où l'homme a noté les minutes décisives de sa vie, minutes joyeuses, minutes tristes, moments solennels ou bizarres' (*1*, p.1098). He evokes the apparently haphazard, fragmentary quality of his writing and, as Dubois suggests, the relief given to particular moments.

Nonetheless, *L'Enfant* takes its place within a clear overall framework, as demonstrated by my outline of the trilogy. Also it is a coherent entity in its own right, given shape and direction by strong central themes. Despite the frequent absence of explicit links both between and within chapters, episodes are sequenced in a readily identifiable chronological development. Chapter headings themselves, 'Ma Mère', 'La Famille', 'Le Collège' etc. indicate a logical outward movement from the nuclear to the extended family, and on to contacts with the outside world. In *Le Bachelier* and *L'Insurgé* landmarks will be essentially historical, but here they are primarily geographical and social. As Jacques moves from the small provincial town of Le Puy to Saint-Etienne, Nantes and finally the capital itself, his repeated physical displacement parallels the broadening of his own horizons, his growing experience and politicization, and culminates in Paris, 'bivouac de la Révolution' (*3*, p.256). At the same time the theme of imprisonment which fuels his revolt is reinforced by the move from open countryside to the hemming in of the industrial agglomeration.

For the greater part of the novel Vallès is sketching in the general atmosphere of Jacques's childhood. From Chapter XXIII onwards, however, when he and his mother are reconciled on new ground in Paris, the structure tightens, con-veying a sequence of developments linked in a clear chain of cause and effect, as we approach the climax of the novel. Rapid shifts of scene now reflect the acceleration in action, as tensions mount and precipitate confrontation. Explicit markers are also

present. Chapter XXIV 'Le Retour' ends with the dramatic fore-
warning: 'L'abîme est creusé', but suspense is shortlived as the
following chapter announces: 'Le malheur est arrivé' (p.397).

Earlier in the novel, references to past and future
developments have helped to illustrate the full significance of
events. In the solemn episode where Monsieur Vingtras stresses
the sanctity of bread, we are made aware of the deep impression
made by his words and the importance they would later assume:
'Tu verras ce qu'il [le pain] vaut. Je l'ai vu' (p.71). Reflecting on
the subject of dishonesty, Jacques comments: 'si la contrefaçon
des exemptions mène au bagne, je devrais y être', and then adds,
almost as an afterthought, set in relief in a single line isolated at
the end of the chapter: 'Et qui dit que je n'irai pas?' (p.151). The
remark clearly anticipates political imprisonment later in the
trilogy. After the Brignolin scandal it is made explicit that we
have reached a turning-point (pp.227-28). The presence of such
pointers suggests the narrator's overview and imposes a sense of
direction. Yet this becomes ever more compelling towards the
end of the novel as surface-markers of this order proliferate and
the forward-looking perspective becomes more dominant. When
he is prevented from running away from boarding school,
Jacques speculates: 'Mais je me suis demandé souvent s'il
n'aurait pas autant valu que je m'échappasse ce jour-là, et qu'il
fût décidé tout de suite que ma vie serait une série de combats?'
(p.343). He points ahead repeatedly to further combat (see
pp.401-02), stressing that *L'Enfant* presents only the first in a
series of struggles. Purged by his duel, in the final pages he
declares: 'j'entre dans la vie d'homme, prêt à la lutte, plein de
force, bien honnête ... Je suis mon maître à partir
d'aujourd'hui. Mon père avait le droit de me frapper ... Mais
malheur maintenant, malheur à qui me touche! — Ah! oui!
malheur à celui-là!' (p.408). He announces the end of an era.
Childhood is brought to a close, but interest is stimulated in the
future.

At the same time symbolic episodes give shape and significance to the trilogy as a whole. The final lines of *L'Insurgé*
depict the sky of Paris, 'd'un bleu cru, avec des nuées rouges.
On dirait une grande blouse inondée de sang'. Intermingled

notions of guilt and expiation, frustration and cathartic liberation run through all three volumes, the duel of *L'Enfant* finding its parallel in the duel with Legrand in *Le Bachelier* and the bloodshed of the Commune at the end of *L'Insurgé*. The theme also gives a sense of form and completion to *L'Enfant* itself, with the introduction of the notion of guilt in the very first chapter when Monsieur Vingtras cuts his finger while making a toy for Jacques, and its expiation in the final chapter. The conciliatory power of bloodshed is anticipated in the meantime when Jacques's wounds from the broken picture frame bring his parents closer together (p.126). The 'coup de couteau' also finds its parallel, for it is in these terms that Jacques describes the blow he receives when forced to return to Nantes to resit his *baccalauréat* (p.376). Bloodshed is the hallmark of his martyrdom. He is not an anaemic melancholic figure, but a victim of full-blooded brutality, who will ultimately respond in kind. His mother beats him till he is raw (pp.39-40). The verb 'saigner' is used to describe his father's punishments (p.196). Yet Jacques is excluded, forbidden to participate in a bloody pub brawl (p.100). More glorious battles, however, are to come, in which he will be able to demonstrate his solidarity: at the end of *L'Enfant*, solidarity with his family; at the end of the trilogy, solidarity with the larger ranks of the oppressed.

Impressionist painters cultivated a style which was by no means a disguise for lack of clarity in vision. Similarly the episodic, anecdotal style of *L'Enfant*, the fragmentation and disruption, in no way imply a lack of sense of direction. The entire fabric of the novel is conceived with the ultimate conflagration of the Commune looming ahead. So, in style, perspective and form, as at every other level, a creative fusion is established between the spirit of revolt and yet an overriding sense of purpose.

6. Conclusion

In my introduction I noted Vallès's paradoxical attitude to literature. Within *L'Enfant* its role is questioned. 'Le Livre' becomes a symbol of authority, called upon to condone parental tyranny (pp.41, 391), and justifying it with historical precedents (pp.297-98). At school it represents the tyranny of past over present, drudgery and mindless repetition (Chapter XX 'Mes Humanités') in contrast to the child's fantasies, his love of nature, freedom and adventure (pp.239, 284). Yet its role is not entirely negative, for a clear opposition emerges between establishment literature, perpetuating the values of bourgeois society, and Jacques's chosen but forbidden reading. The most impassioned passages of the novel are inspired by adventure stories enjoyed in secret. They provide a cherished refuge for a troubled and impressionable child. Jacques enthuses over tales of fishing (pp.67-68, 72), the adventures of Captain Cook (pp.72-73), Robinson Crusoe (pp.144-49), even Napoleon (pp.178-79), and is driven to forgery in order to acquire such books (pp.149-51). Yet in doing so he himself becomes a 'victime du livre', illustrating the dangers Vallès had highlighted in his article of this title. Jacques's reactions are dominated by his reading: 'Je dis: "ô ma mère!" sans y penser beaucoup, c'est pour faire comme dans les livres' (p.146). He allows himself to be fettered and duped, 'comme un perroquet enchaîné au grand mât' (pp.241-42). The dangers of romantic literature are evident in the distance established between fiction and reality. Jacques's arrival in Nantes is a great disappointment to him, for all his illusions about the seafaring life (pp.241-42) are shattered by the dull provincial town (pp.264-66).

In contrast the positive catalytic force which realist writing may exert is demonstrated when literature on the history of the Revolution, focusing on ordinary people with whom Jacques can identify, transforms his life, and makes a revolutionary of the rebel (pp.370-72). Significantly the seafaring metaphors of adventure stories re-emerge here in a new context, to convey the excitement of the printing-shop (pp.373-74). It is not through romantic escapism but by allying himself with the working-classes and fighting for their cause that Jacques will win his freedom. But why is it specifically in a printing-shop that he longs to work? Unlike predecessors in this ambition, such as Balzac, Jacques's chief desire is to become a manual worker. Yet his particular choice of trade also demonstrates the fascination literature holds for him, and equally the importance of the nature of the communication it effects. In this case it is a news-paper which is being printed. The attraction lies not only in involvement in a productive task, but in the nature of journalism itself, in so far as it may represent a form of realist literature which keeps abreast with changes in contemporary society, espouses causes and reflects and informs the lives of ordinary people.

The preferences expressed by Jacques are reflected in the nature of *L'Enfant* itself, for its writing owes much to Vallès's experience as a journalist, as demonstrated in our discussion of style. On the thematic level Vallès takes up specific causes which can be traced in his journalism too. Undeniably he conforms to his own criteria for realism in drawing his inspiration exclusively from personal experience of contemporary reality. He also avoids the 'Tyrannie comique de l'Imprimé' by constant dis-ruption and subversion, stimulating the reader's critical faculties. Conformism is replaced by irreverence, tyranny by contention. Jacques, as narrator, far from setting himself up as an authority, is the first to admit his own limitations and falli-bility. Thus, in literary creation itself, Vallès resolves the con-flicting tensions which inspire his ambivalent attitude to the printed word.

Select Bibliography

A. VALLES'S WRITING

The trilogy is available in Livre de Poche, Garnier-Flammarion and Collection Folio editions, but for consistency all references are drawn from the last. The Pléiade edition of Vallès's works is my second source of reference, but as the first volume only has been published to date, the reader is also referred to the widest selection of Vallès's writing currently available: *Les Œuvres complètes de Jules Vallès*, edited by Lucien Scheler (Paris, Les Editeurs Français Réunis [E.F.R. hereafter], 1950-73) 15 vols. Only volumes of this edition referred to in the text are detailed below, but the entire collection should be consulted for an overall view of the range and character of Vallès's writing.

1. *Jules Vallès, Œuvres I, 1857-1870*, ed. by Roger Bellet, Bibliothèque de la Pléiade (Gallimard, 1975).
2. *Le Bachelier*, pref. by Michel Tournier, Collection Folio (Gallimard, 1974).
3. *L'Insurgé*, pref. by Marie-Claire Bancquart, Collection Folio (Gallimard, 1975).
4. *Le Proscrit, Correspondance avec Arthur Arnould, 1852-1880*, ed. by L. Scheler, 2nd ed. (E.F.R., 1973).
5. *Correspondance avec Hector Malot*, ed. by M.-C. Bancquart (E.F.R., 1968).
6. *Un Gentilhomme, Les Blouses*, prefaces by L. Scheler and Jean Dautry (E.F.R., 1957).
7. *Souvenirs d'un étudiant pauvre, Le Candidat des pauvres, Lettre à Jules Mirès*, pref. by L. Scheler, notes by M.-C. Bancquart and L. Scheler (E.F.R., 1972).
8. *Littérature et révolution, recueil de textes littéraires*, ed. by R. Bellet (E.F.R., 1969).
9. *Œuvres complètes, 4 vols* (Paris, Les Editeurs Français Réunis et Livre Club Diderot, 1969-70) — less scholarly than the Pléiade or E.F.R. editions, but reproduces texts which they omit.
10. *Le Bachelier* (University of London Press, 1972) — particularly helpful to the English student, thanks to the chronology, introduction and notes by Walter D. Redfern.

B. CRITICAL WORKS

Books

11. Bancquart, M.C., *Jules Vallès* (Paris, Seghers, 1971) — sound general introduction to the man and writer.

12. Bellet, R., *Jules Vallès journaliste du IIe Empire, de la Commune de Paris et de la IIIe République (1857-1885)* (E.F.R., 1977) — excellent thesis by the man responsible for the Pléiade edition of Vallès's work, currently regarded as the leading scholar on Vallès.

13. Bonnefis, Philippe, *Jules Vallès: du bon usage de la lame et de l'aiguille* (Lausanne, L'Age d'Homme, Cistre-Essai 13, 1982) — psychoanalytical reading, recommended only for the ambitious.

14. Brombert, Victor H., 'Vallès and the pathos of rebellion' in *The Intellectual Hero: studies in the French novel, 1880-1955* (London, Faber, 1962), pp.43-51.

15. *Colloque Jules Vallès* (Presses Universitaires de Lyon, 1975) — contains some of the most interesting articles on *L'Enfant* published to date.

16. Delforge, Christiane, *L'Art de Jules Vallès dans 'Jacques Vingtras'* (Université de Bruxelles, Thèse Lettres, 1930).

17. Dubois, Jacques, *Les Romanciers français de l'instantané* (Bruxelles, Palais des Académies, 1963).

18. Giaufret Colombani, Hélène, *Rhétorique de Jules Vallès: les figures de la dénomination et de l'analogie dans 'L'Enfant'* (Geneva, Slatkine, 1984) — detailed and sophisticated analysis.

19. Gille, Gaston, *Jules Vallès (1832-1885): ses révoltes, sa maîtrise, son prestige* (Paris, Flammarion, 1941; reprinted Geneva, Slatkine, 1981) — still the broadest, most comprehensive study of the writer and his work.

20. ——, *Jules Vallès: sources, bibliographie et iconographie* (Paris, Flammarion, 1941; reprinted Geneva, Slatkine, 1981) — an invaluable reference work.

21. Lejeune, Philippe, 'Le récit d'enfance ironique: Vallès', in *Je est un autre: l'autobiographie de la littérature aux médias* (Paris, Seuil, 1980), pp.10-31 — indispensable reading.

22. Lockshin, Janine E., *Jules Vallès romancier: étude de la trilogie* (Ph.D. thesis, Univ. of Rochester, 1975). Available from University Microfilms International (Ann Arbor, Michigan, 1983).

23. Pillu, Pierre, *Jules Vallès, 'L'Enfant', 'Le Bachelier', 'L'Insurgé'*, extracts and critical notes (Paris, Bordas, 1974).

24. *Revue d'études vallésiennes*. New review published by 'Les Amis de Jules Vallès'. First number (Dec. 1984) contains articles on the trilogy and childhood in particular. Second number (Oct. 1985) contains proceedings of the 'Colloque Jules Vallès' in Saint-Etienne, March 1985, amongst which are many excellent papers.

25. Rollin, Renée H., *The Comic Spirit in the Trilogy of Jules Vallès* (Ph.D. thesis, Bryn Mawr College, 1976). Available from University Microfilms International (Ann Arbor, Michigan, 1983).

Articles

26. Bellet, R., 'Littérature et société selon Jules Vallès, 1865-85', *Europe*, no.431-32 (March-April, 1965), pp.238-47.

27. ——, 'Jules Vallès et le compagnonnage', *Europe*, no.616-17 (Aug.-Sept., 1980), pp.184-91.

28. ——, 'Jules Vallès et son Velay', in *Mélanges offerts à George Contry* (Lyon, Nov. 1982), pp.551-62.

29. Dubois, J., 'La caricature d'une société dans *L'Enfant* de Jules Vallès', *Revue des Langues Vivantes* (24ᵉ année, no.5, 1958), pp.373-76.

30. ——, 'Une page de *L'Enfant* de Jules Vallès', *Cahiers d'Analyse Textuelle* (no.2, 1960), pp.61-67.

31. Nikolov, B., 'Le lexique populaire dans l'œuvre de Jules Vallès', *Annuaire de l'Université de Sofia* (Faculté Philologique, vol.LV, 2, 1961), pp.119-322.

32. ——, 'Les néologismes dans l'œuvre de Jules Vallès', *Annuaire de l'Université de Sofia* (Faculté des Lettres, vol.LXV, 1, 1971), pp.1-51.

33. Redfern, W.D., 'Delinquent parents: Jules Vallès and *L'Enfant*', *Mosaic*, V, 3, 1972 (University of Manitoba Press), pp.167-77.

34. ——, 'Le Jeu de mots dans la trilogie de Vallès', *Europe*, no.528 (April, 1973), pp.175-85.

35. ——, 'Vallès and the existential pun', *Mosaic*, IX, 3, April 1976 (University of Manitoba Press), pp.27-39.

CRITICAL GUIDES TO FRENCH TEXTS

edited by

Roger Little, Wolfgang van Emden, David Williams